W9-BUL-637

Ex Libris
© APCo

THE FOLIAGE GARDEN

TAPESTRIES OF COLOR, SHAPE, AND TEXTURE

BECKE DAVIS

FRIEDMAN/FAIRFAX
PUBLISHERS

DEDICATION AND ACKNOWLEDGMENTS

To Marty, Jessica, and Jonathan
To friends and neighbors, old and new—
To volunteers everywhere, especially
those in Promiseland and Summerside P.T.O.
To educators everywhere
To everyone who would really like
a tree for their birthday, but was afraid to ask
To Susan Lauzau, for giving me this opportunity
to make new gardening friends
And in memory of Linda Louise McCartney
and Edith Sarah Davis Adams

To every gardener who ever rushed to check out the beautiful fall-colored vine climbing up a tree, only to discover it was poison ivy—the ability to laugh at yourself and not take yourself too seriously is one of the first requirements of gardening.

A FRIEDMAN/FAIRFAX BOOK

Library of Congress Cataloging-in-Publication data available upon request.

ISBN 1-56799-696-5

Editor: Susan Lauzau
Art Director: Jeff Batzli
Designer: Jan Melchior
Photography Editor: Valerie E. Kennedy
Production Manager: Jeanne E. Hutter

Color separations by Fine Arts Repro House Co., Ltd.
Printed in England by Butler & Tanner Limited

1 3 5 7 9 10 8 6 4 2

For bulk purchases and special sales, please contact:
Friedman/Fairfax Publishers
Attention: Sales Department
15 West 26th Street
New York, New York 10010
212/685-6610 FAX 212/685-1307

Visit our website:
http://www.metrobooks.com

CONTENTS

INTRODUCTION

OPPOSITE: ***A lush garden of hostas and ferns glows deep emerald in the dappled shade. Plants with colored, textured, or beautifully shaped foliage provide interest throughout the year, whether or not the plant is in flower.***

Some are born gardening, some seek to garden, and others have gardening thrust upon them. To some people, gardening is something that you do. To others, like myself, gardening is a way of life, not so much describing what we do as defining who we are. In the same way, to some people, gardening is about flowers. When you become immersed in gardening—really get into the spirit of it—it has a wonderful way of seeping into every aspect of daily life, teaching patience where there was none, showing connection and intention instead of isolation and accident. Working with plants and soil teaches one to take satisfaction in the accomplishment of the day, while staying open to the requirements of the future and learning from the experiences of the past.

Gardening at this level is a sort of dirt-under-the-fingernails transcendental meditation; it's about transcending the mundane without crossing over into the merely wacky, and encouraging meditation about the small miracles that occur in the garden every day. Gardening helps us keep reality in focus. It enables us to connect with an immense universe through the tiniest leaf of the tiniest plant.

It's a soppy metaphor, but think of a young couple in love for the first time. It's all ooh's and aah's and pretty girls and hunky guys showing off their finery at the senior prom. All that prettiness is like a garden full of flowers at the peak of its bloom—brilliant colors, beautiful flowers, breathtaking altogether. There's nothing wrong with prettiness or flowers, but as gardeners grow into the spirit of gardening they want to learn more, understand more, and get to know the plants at a deeper level. We start to investigate soil types, microclimates, and pests and diseases. We learn about cultivars, hybrids, and plant families. As we start to find out what our plants need to grow and thrive, the ephemeral flowers become just another part of the plant as a whole. The flowers, after all, are only at their prime for a few weeks while the foliage can be interesting for most of the year. Fruit, bark, and seedheads suddenly seem as attractive as the flowers. Before you know it, there is an understanding between you and the plants that transcends small talk and pretty faces. In a sense you are married to the garden, to the soil and all the living

things that form a living connection, like an electrical current between you and the plants you cultivate.

Foliage is more than leaves on a stem. It is the texture and the detail that carries a garden from mere prettiness to a more serene and lasting beauty. Every leaf, front and back, is a finely detailed work of art. The appreciation of foliage comes gradually but inevitably, the way a person who gardens gradually and inevitably becomes one with the garden.

Chapter 1

A Close-Up Look at Leaves

Most people are familiar with the expression "you can't see the forest for the trees." In fact, many people don't really see trees at all—trees are just part of the background, part of the scenery. Even less likely to be noticed are the leaves on the trees, the needles on evergreens, or spiky fronds of ornamental grasses. If it wasn't for brightly colored flowers and vividly green grass, some people would hardly notice the plants growing around them at all.

*The glossy green foliage of European wild ginger (*Asarum europaeum*) makes it a standout in a shady woodland garden. It is an excellent groundcover when planted in small clumps at the base of a tree.*

A good way to get to know leaves is to work on a leaf identification project. In our neighborhood, autumn is leaf collection time at several local schools. Handy little guide books take kids and their parents step-by-step through a maze of leaf descriptions. There are leaf books and field guides that describe leaves by texture and shape, by autumn color, by seed and flower, and by bark, bud, and stem. Whether you have children or not, a leaf collection can be an excellent learning experience. It can also drive you completely nuts.

Both my kids have learned a lot from leaf collections, but I have learned even more. First, it is a lot easier to identify a leaf when the tree is in front of you. Second, the secret is in the details—when all the leaves start to look the same, take note of the shape of the bud, the direction of the veining, the texture of the underside of the leaf. Third, leaves are not quite as diverse as snowflakes, but they are not formed from die-cuts, either. You think you know what a maple leaf looks like? Guess again. My kids confidently identify leaves while I hover doubtfully checking their decisions. A few of our trees have even stumped the experts.

For instance, one newly purchased sweet gum (*Liquidambar styraciflua*), obtained from a reliable supplier, is so young that there is not much bark to check. What bark there exists is greeny-gray, and parts of it are corky. The buds are pointy, and the leaf color is green, with mottled orange, red, and yellow autumn color. The leaf shapes are something else again. At the top of the tree they look pretty much like typical sweet gum leaves—not quite the star shape I carry in my mind's eye, but close. Further down the trunk, though, the leaves look more and more like maple leaves. Leaves on the lowest branches are virtually the same shape as a red maple, but they are alternate like a sweet gum, instead of opposite, like a maple. Looking through my reference books, the top leaves are reminiscent of the hedge maple, *Acer campestre*, which also can have corky bark. I'd say I have a sweet gum, but you'd never convince anyone by its leaves alone. Even area experts are bewildered.

Some trees, like sassafras and mulberry, are known for their variable leaves. Others, like catalpa, are easily recognized by their large leaves and interesting seedpods. Some hawthorns and locusts can be spotted by their thorns, and shagbark hickory is readily identified by its shaggy bark. The object of leaf identification is not just to give you or your child a rudimentary knowledge of trees and their leaves, it is also to open your eyes to the little things, sharpening your focus on leaves with finely serrated edges, silvery underbellies, or napping of velvety down. In order to really appreciate foliage, it is first necessary to train your eyes to see it.

Look at the way young children draw trees—a big brown trunk topped by a circle of green. A Christmas tree is an A-shaped brown stick dressed in green. By the time children are older, they have added branches, individual leaves, or even a semblance of needles. In much the same way, as the vision of a gardener matures, the close-up details of a leaf take on more significance. A leaf collection, culled from fallen leaves with permission from the property owners, can be the first step through the looking-glass and into a foliage wonderland.

The leaves of some plants are so interesting and unusual that artists seem drawn to use them in paintings, photographs, wood carvings, and textiles. Fan-shaped ginkgo leaves are often found in fabric and wallpaper designs, as well as in jewelry motifs. The shape and color of maple and oak leaves are also frequently found in home furnishings and clothing fabrics. In Victorian times, the leaves of perennial bear's breeches (*Acanthus mollis*) were repeated throughout the home, and today everything from tableware to picture frames can be found embellished with leaf designs. Leaves, flowers, and seedpods are frequently dried and used in flower arrangements, bringing the garden inside even in winter. Besides garlands of pine and spruce, the distinctive leaves of ivy and holly are almost synonymous with winter

OPPOSITE TOP: ***The ridged, heart-shaped leaves of sweet violet (*****Viola odorata*****) complement the tiny flowers and form a neat, dark green nosegay when the blooms have gone.*** OPPOSITE BOTTOM: ***The finely cut leaves of common squirrel corn (*****Dicentra canadensis*****) are every bit as ornamental as the flowers on this North American native. It is easy to picture the leaf pattern translated to wallpaper or a classic upholstery design.***

ABOVE LEFT: ***Ghostweed or snow-on-the-mountain (*****Euphorbia marginata*****), a North American native, has striking foliage that makes it popular—if hard to find—for garden use. Wear gloves or long sleeves when handling it, though, especially on sunny days, because it can cause severe dermatitis or photo-dermatitis.*** ABOVE RIGHT: ***Who says a garden needs flowers to be colorful? This artful arrangement of common germander (*****Teucrium chamaedrys*****), the silvery leaves of lavender cotton (*****Santolina** ***spp.) and the brilliant gold, tiny leaves of*** **Origanum vulgare** ***'Aureum' doesn't need flowers to be a standout.***

holiday decorations. The fragrant leaves of eucalyptus, silvery, cut-leaf artemisia foliage, and the fuzzy stems of pussy willow also bring nature indoors.

Foliage is a key design consideration outside the home, as well. When designing a landscape, it is important to consider the size and shape of any trees because their ultimate height, width, and form will make a dramatic impact on the final result.

It can be equally important to the overall landscape design to consider the size and shape of your plants' individual leaves. The small, compound leaves of a honeylocust provide filtered shade and a soft, almost feathery texture. The oversized leaves of a catalpa, accompanied by their string bean–type seedpods, are a standout in any landscape. Tuliptrees have leaves that are sometimes described as maple leaves with the tops cut off, while sycamores dominate the landscape with their immense size and by the equally dramatic size of their leaves.

The leaves of oakleaf hydrangea are as interesting to me as the flower heads that give hydrangeas their claim to fame. The heart-shaped leaves of a redbud and the more rounded, ridged leaves of a flowering dogwood may not be as eyecatching as their flowers, but they provide interest for a much longer period. The leaves of sweet gum (*Liquidambar styraciflua*) are almost perfect star shapes, green in summer and beautifully mottled in autumn. The leaves of 'Big Daddy' hosta open into a curved cup shape, while the foliage of lady's mantle (*Alchemilla mollis*) is just curved enough to capture dewdrops.

From the great straplike leaves of cannas to the delicate foliage of a fernleaf peony, there is virtually no design that cannot be found in nature. Think of your landscape as an extension of your home, and weave foliage patterns in natural designs the same way you would incorporate designs from nature into your home.

Foliage Forms and Descriptions

When identifying leaves, it helps to have a general knowledge of the terminology used by horticulturists and botanists to describe the characteristics of each leaf. These are not words you have to memorize—most will not come up in everyday conversation. They will, however, help you understand the leaf descriptions used in many reference books, field guides, and garden catalogs. The terms listed here apply primarily to leaves—it would take several pages to list additional terms that describe flowers, seeds, roots, and other parts of the plant—and it should be considered a brief guide rather than a complete glossary.

Texture

Some terms that describe the texture of a leaf's surface are *pubescent* (covered in soft, fine, downy hairs), *villous* (like pubescent, but with longer and shaggier hairs), *tomentose* (dense, rigid, tight, short hairs), *velutinous* (similar to tomentose but denser and more velvety), *pannose* (also dense but feeling more like felt), *squamose* (scaly), *papillose* (covered in tiny, round bumps), and *floccose* (dense tufts of hair). Other textural descriptions include *hirsute* (covered in long hairs), *scabrous* (rough, tiny bristles or hairs), *rugose* (wrinkled), *glabrous* (smooth and hairless), and *lustrous* (shiny).

ABOVE: ***The leaves of mayapple* (Podophyllum peltatum*), also called mandrake, have five to nine palmate lobes which, as the botanical name indicates, are "peltate"—meaning that the stalk of the plant is not joined to the leaf at the edge but, in this case, at the leaf's center.***

Veins and Lobes

Lobing characteristics, the "cut edge" look of a leaf, can help narrow down a particular species within a genus. The veining of a leaf may generally go unnoticed, but the pattern of the veins can provide a sort of fingerprint to narrow down identification. Terms to describe the type of lobing on a leaf include *palmate* (three or more lobes rising from the same point, like a palm or fingers splayed), *cleft* (a lobe that is cut to about the middle), *lobed* (divided segments of a leaf, usually rounded), and *pinnatisect* (deeply cut lobes, almost cut to the mid-rib of the leaf). Veins may be *prominent* (visible, standing out from the surface), *pinnate* (featherlike), *reticulate* (a close or open network of veins that connect at one point), or *ribbed* (with prominent veins), to name a few.

Margins

The margins, or edges, of leaves can be very distinctive—sometimes a small detail like the direction the tip of the leaf points can be the main clue to its identity. A margin that is *dentate* features triangle-shaped shallow teeth. A *denticulate* margin is similar to a dentate edge, but with lots of tiny teeth instead of a few large ones. The term *serrate* may be familiar because it describes the edge of a common kitchen knife. When used to describe a leaf margin it denotes a sharp, sawlike edge, usually curving forward. A leaf that is *biserrate* has a smaller saw-tooth edge between each of the primary saw "teeth." Think of parsley for an example of a *crispate* leaf with irregularly curled edges. Think scalloped for *crenate* and finely scalloped for *crenulate*. An *incised* leaf edge is deeply cut, while

ABOVE LEFT: ***Look no further than the vegetable garden for some of the most interesting foliage around. Here 'White Sprouting' broccoli and 'Rubine Red' and 'Bedford' brussels sprouts await winter harvest.*** ABOVE CENTER: ***Red New Zealand flax (*****Phormium tenax*****) makes a bold statement that could work equally well in a mixed planting or as a specimen in a container.*** ABOVE RIGHT: ***Bear's breeches (*****Acanthus*** ***spp.) is one of the lethal weapons of the perennial world. The spineless foliage of common bear's breeches (*****Acanthus mollis*****) was a popular motif in ancient Greece, but the spiky leaves of spiny bear's breeches (*****Acanthus spinosus*** ***and "spinossimus" types) make a distinctive, if dangerous, addition to any foliage garden.***

a *laciniate* edge is more deeply and sharply cut. A leaf that is *entire* has no lobes or teeth to interrupt the smooth lines of its margin, while an *undulate* leaf is smooth but wavy.

Compound Leaves

Compound leaves are composed of two or more leaflets. The way that the plant's individual leaflets are arranged on the twig is either going to be *opposite* (leaves on either side of the twig lined up evenly so the leaves meet at the base) or *alternate* (leaves staggered in so that they alternate in placement along the twig). The following terms describe the arrangement of the leaflets that make up the compound leaf, rather than the shape of each individual leaflet.

A *pinnate* compound leaf has rows of leaflets arranged something like a feather; *imparipinnate* describes a pinnate compound leaf that has a single leaflet at the top or end of the leaf. The pinnate leaflets may break off into twos (*bipinnate*) or even into threes (*tripinnate*). A compound leaf with three leaflets is called *trifoliolate*; a compound leaf with all its leaflets originating at the same point in a fingerlike fan pattern is described as *digitate*.

Simple Leaves

A simple leaf is complete in itself, without breaking off into leaflets. The distinctive shape of a gingko leaf is described as *flabellate*, while a leaf that is long, narrow and spearlike is called *lanceolate*. A leaf that is more like an arrow than a spear is called *sagittate*. A heart-shaped leaf, pointed at the top, is described as *cordate*; a heart-shaped leaf, pointed at the base, is called *obcordate*. A triangular leaf that is attached at the broad base is called *deltoid*; a kidney-shaped leaf is described as *reniform* and a basically diamond-shaped leaf is called *rhomboidal*. Long, slim grassy stems may be described as *linear*; an *ensiform* leaf is shaped like a sword that comes to a sharp point.

There are many more types and shapes of leaves than these, but they are most likely unnecessary for a home gardener. Use the set of terms as a starting point so that when you come across these descriptions, you will be able to call up a mental image of the corresponding shape.

ABOVE: ***Colorful herbs have been used to create this traditional and highly decorative knot garden. Patterns for this type of garden are as varied as the gardener's imagination—ancient knot gardens were often copied from intricate lace designs. Herbs are well suited to knot gardens because most are very adaptable to clipping and shearing.***

ABOVE: ***Brilliant bark, delicate foliage form, and fresh leaf color would earn this Japanese maple*** **(Acer palmatum)** ***a prime place in any foliage garden.***

ABOVE: ***The tiny heart-shaped leaves of epimedium (*****Epimedium*** ***spp.), also known as bishop's hat, form clusters that can make an effective groundcover for dry shade.***

LARGE TROUGH GARDEN

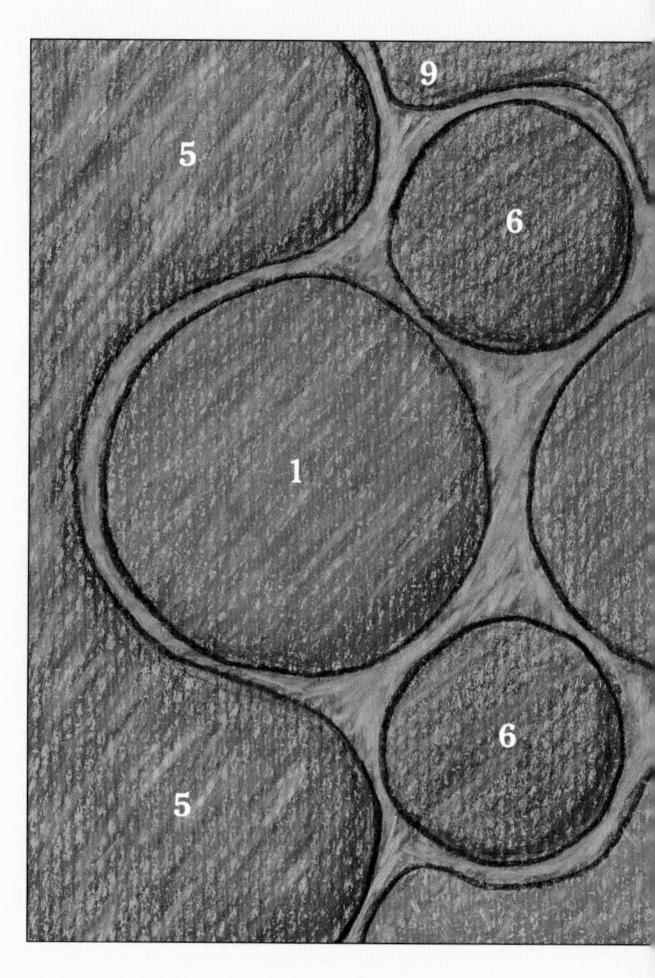

This trough garden plan can easily be adapted for a raised bed, if that is more suitable for your overall garden design. The trough may be an old sink or tub, a hollow stone, or a purchased container of any variety of materials. Whatever material you use, try painting the surface with a mixture of plain yogurt and water to encourage the growth of mosses. A raised bed can be easily created using landscape timbers, rough, flat stones, or even prefabricated materials with the appearance of wood. For handicapped gardeners, the bed can be raised to an accessible level, with wide boards affixed to the top for seating or for setting garden tools and a pitcher of lemonade.

Mix topsoil with organic materials such as compost or shredded leaf mulch, along with sand or grit from finely ground stone (one precaution—if the finely ground stone is limestone, it may make the planting mixture excessively alkaline). I would also toss in some polymer "crystals" that will retain water if the weather is dry. A lighter-weight planting mix with vermiculite could be substituted in small-scale troughs or planters. Keep the soil level at a few inches below the level of the trough or raised bed so it will not overflow in a rainstorm.

This plan is a kind of glorified rock garden, featuring several compact and creeping plants that will benefit from being raised closer to eye level. The common bugleweed is a pretty plant when contained in one place; the foliage of the cultivar 'Burgundy Glow' is attractive, almost surpassing the flowers. Herbs that are both useful and ornamental are used in this garden plan: pot marjoram, creeping thyme, and the subtle but very effective purple sage.

Most gardeners have grown a campanula or two, but not many have tried the trailing or Serbian bellflower. It is getting easier to find in mail-order catalogues (at least, it is no longer impossible), but even if it takes a little trouble, try to find this particular plant instead of substituting the easily found 'Blue Chips' campanula. Like other "Serbians" (spruce, etc.), this bellflower is tough enough to survive even Chicago's unpredictable, but always extreme, winter weather. The little plant *Veronica spicata* 'Blauteppich' may be difficult to find in local nurseries but it is available through several mail-order catalogues. I have yet to find a veronica I didn't like, but this one is truly special.

Coral bells are the continuing thread that runs through this garden plan, mainly because they have so much to offer and so many exciting new cultivars are becoming available. Whether they are hybrid coral bells (*Heuchera* spp.) or hybrids of coral bells and foamflowers

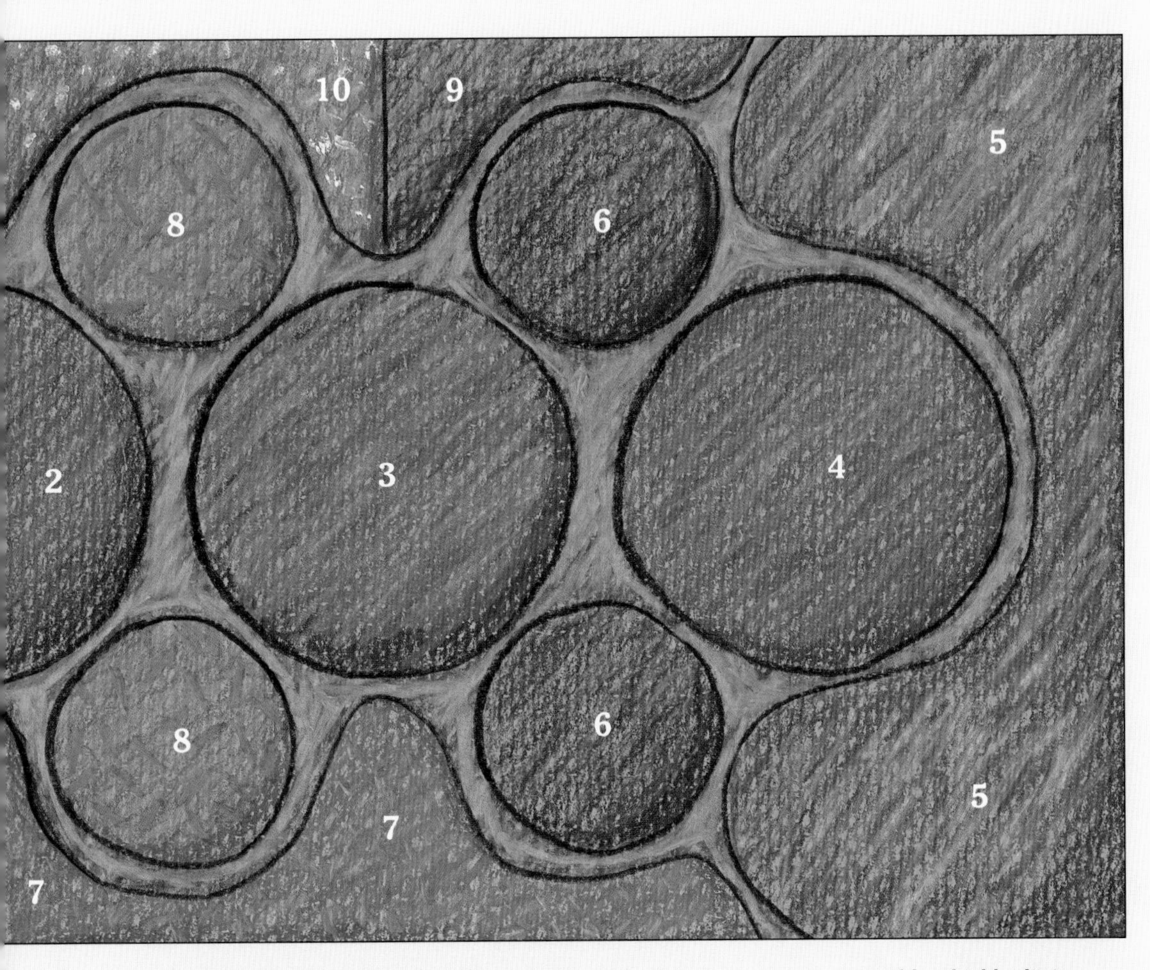

(× *Heucherella* cultivars), these plants have one thing in common—varied but highly distinctive foliage, usually borne in neat mounds topped by tiny flowers that wave on delicate fronds high above the foliage. 'Palace Purple', a cultivar that originated at London's Kew Gardens, is well known for its deep bronze-purple foliage and ivory flowers. The cultivars featured here are just as distinctive but much less common—if they turn out to be too hard to find, don't hesitate to substitute another cultivar with outstanding foliage. With all of these hybrids, foliage steals the show, but the flowers are also an attraction. Don't be shy—even with a raised bed or trough, you may want to kneel down and take a closer look at these small wonders.

PLANT LIST

SUGGESTED QUANTITIES ARE NOTED AFTER EACH PLANT NAME.

1. *Heuchera americana* 'Pewter Veil' (coral bells hybrid)—1
2. *Heuchera americana* 'Amethyst Mist' (coral bells hybrid)—1
3. *Heucherella* × 'Silver Streak' (hybrid of foamflower and coral bells)—1
4. *Heuchera americana* 'Plum Pudding' (coral bells hybrid)—1
5. *Ajuga reptans* 'Burgundy Glow' (bugleweed)—12
6. *Salvia officinalis* 'Purpurascens' (purple sage)—2
7. *Campanula poscharskyana* (Serbian bellflower)—6
8. *Veronica spicata* 'Blauteppich' (spike speedwell)—4
9. *Thymus serpyllum* (creeping thyme)—4
10. *Origanum vulgare* 'Compactum' (pot marjoram)—2

ABOVE: ***A densely packed container emphasizes the thick, succulent foliage of hens-and-chicks*** (Sempervivum ***spp.), while a thick groundcover of English ivy*** (Hedera helix) ***creeps up around the garden ornaments to lend a touch of mystery to the scene.***

Leaves with Distinctive Textures

The first impression of a garden is almost certain to be visual, but in my opinion a garden should be tempting to all the senses. It can be fun to include plants with a variety of textures, from soft and fuzzy to sharp and spiky. Slippery-smooth leaves can feel like satin, while other leaves can be rough and leathery. Whether you are looking for leaves you love to touch or formidable thorny barriers, the plants listed below include a tapestry of textures.

Acanthus spinosus (shiny bear's breeches)—shiny, spiny, leathery

Ajuga spp. (bugleweed)—shiny, corrugated

Artemisia schmidtiana 'Silver Mound' (wormwood)—soft, velvety

Asarum europaeum (shiny-leaf ginger)—smooth, shiny

Bergenia cordifolia (heartleaf bergenia)—fleshy, shiny, thick

Brassica oleracea (ornamental kale)—thick, curled, veined

Cynara cardunculus (cardoon)—woolly, leathery, spiny

Echinops ritro (small globe thistle)—spiny, spiky

Eryngium amethystinum (amethyst sea holly)—spiky

Eryngium bourgatii 'Oxford Blue' (Mediterranean sea holly)—spiky

Hosta montana var. *macrophylla* (hosta, plantain lily)—deeply furrowed

Hosta sieboldiana (hosta, plantain lily)—large, thick, deeply grooved, rugose

Ilex spp. (most hollies)—sharp, spiky

Kochia scoparia forma *trichophylla* (firebush)—feathery

Magnolia grandiflora (southern magnolia)—thick, shiny

Magnolia virginiana (sweetbay magnolia)—smooth, lustrous

Mahonia aquifolium (Oregon grapeholly)—spiny

Onopordum acanthium (giant thistle)—sharp, spiky

Phormium tenax (New Zealand flax—not hardy)—sword-like

Prunus laurocerasus (cherry laurel)—smooth, glossy

Sedum spectabile (showy stonecrop)—thick, fleshy

Sempervivum tectorum (hens-and-chicks)—succulent, sharp points

Stachys byzantina (lamb's ear)—velvety

Stachys macrantha (big betony)—heavy, hairy, wrinkly

Symphytum grandiflorum (groundcover comfrey)—bristly

Yucca filamentosa (Adam's needle)—sharp, swordlike

BELOW LEFT: ***Lamb's ears (*****Stachys byzantina*****) feel plush and velvety.*** BELOW RIGHT: ***Bugleweed (*****Ajuga genovensis*****) has shiny, deeply veined leaves.***

ABOVE: *'Silver King' artemisia (*Artemisia ludoviciana *'Silver King') is heat- and drought-tolerant and easy to grow. The tall, silvery foliage makes a stunning accent, but be careful of its tendency to spread out of bounds.*

LEFT: ***Perfect for a rock garden or planting trough, a colorful mix of stonecrop (*Sedum *spp.) and hens-and-chicks (*Sempervivum *spp.) can be just as interesting as traditional flowers, but they look attractive for a longer period.***

RIGHT: ***The multicolored leaves of bugleweed (*Ajuga *spp.) form a dense carpet of foliage that, in ideal planting conditions, can be hard to restrain. Hybrids and cultivars such as 'Burgundy Glow' (shown here) look great on their own or mixed together.***

CHAPTER 2

Bud Break: The Leaves of Spring

I WAS BORN IN APRIL, AND I HAVE NEVER BEEN SURE HOW MUCH OF MY EAGER ANTICIPATION OF SPRING'S ARRIVAL DATES BACK TO MY CHILDHOOD, WHEN I UNDOUBTEDLY COUNTED THE DAYS UNTIL MY BIRTHDAY. TIMES CHANGE AND NOWADAYS I WOULD JUST AS SOON FORGET ABOUT BIRTHDAYS, BUT I STILL FIND AN INNER EXCITEMENT BUILDING AS THE DAYS LENGTHEN AND THE TEMPERATURES RISE. I FIND MY EXCITEMENT BUILDS IN STAGES—STEP ONE COMES SHORTLY AFTER THE NEW YEAR, WHEN IT DAWNS ON ME THAT I AM WITNESSING A FEW MORE MINUTES OF LIGHT EVERY DAY.

This tableau is rich with texture and color: the thick, seersucker leaves of a blue sieboldiana-type hosta and the rich burgundy hues of a velvety coleus are set off by arching branches of brightly variegated foliage.

Step two is when I visit the Cincinnati Nature Center and find the snow melting to reveal countless thousands of winter aconites and snowdrops. The Nature Center is over 200 acres (80ha), and it does my soul good to see that first flush of spring color, almost as far as the eye can see. In addition to the bulbs, I can't help but notice the spidery flowers of witch hazel, and the fuzzy buds of assorted magnolias. Maple, oak, beech, hickory, and of course Ohio's buckeye can be found along the paths. The emerging red buds of the red maples and the unfurling leaves of beech and buckeye are another sign that spring is near. In the clear, cold daylight of very early spring, the different patterns of bark seem highlighted in sharp relief. Even bark that normally does not have ornamental value can capture my attention before the leaves appear. Deeply ridged cottonwoods, peeling shagbark hickories, the furrowed bark of American elms, and the pale, smooth bark of American beeches—each as distinct and interesting as a fingerprint. The bark of a black cherry is rough, with little to commend it, but the bark of a sweet cherry is smoother and more ornamental, while the bark of the amur chokecherry (*Prunus maacki*) is stunning.

By the time the tiny shoots of crocuses and grape hyacinths have appeared—step three—I no longer am in doubt that spring has arrived. At home I favor small daffodils, but who can fail to be impressed when the thousands of tall trumpet daffodils that fill the woods and roadsides of the Nature Center burst into bright yellow bloom? The different varieties open over a period of weeks so it seems they are blooming forever. The drooping catkins on alders, filberts, and birches, the fuzzy "flowers" of green ash that appear before the leaves as well as the grotesque outcrops of fungi—in the last weeks before bud break, everything in nature seems brighter and more interesting.

As April comes to Cincinnati, a mass of white blossoms burst into bloom—pear trees, crabapples, serviceberries, white fringetrees,

RIGHT: ***A shaft of sunlight lends a touch of magic to a glade of ferns in this richly textured shade garden. The composition is an interesting balance of ostrich fern (*Matteuccia struthiopteris*), hostas, the palmate leaves of *Rodgersia podophylla*, and hybrid skunk cabbage (*Lysichiton *spp.*).***

star magnolias, koreanspice viburnums—white, and white edged with pink, seems to be everywhere. Silvery artemisia and velvety lamb's ears appear from out of nowhere, while the spikes of ornamental grasses emerge in welcome clumps of green. Ault Park, the site of Cincinnati's annual flower show, looks like it has been decorated for a wedding, but it is all nature's doing. Well, a few handily placed gardeners might have helped. Tulips and peonies are everywhere, and pansies appear by the bucketful. The woods that cover the nearby hills seem to change from winter gray to a softer beige, then, leaf by leaf, the hills begin to show a flush of green.

Step four. I wake up one morning to find that the grass is green and leaves seem to have covered the neighborhood trees overnight. I know that nature works slowly, but it always seems to sneak up on me overnight, even though I have been eagerly waiting for this moment for months. Grasslike liriope emerges, along with lamium and lavender. Lily of the valley leaves unfurl along with hostas, as the azaleas start to shine.

Spring is here.

ABOVE: ***The tiny golden leaves of an 'Aurea' red oak*** **(Quercus rubra** ***'Aurea') uncurl slowly in anticipation of warm weather.***

PLANTS TO START THE SEASON

There is a telltale warmth in the air. The days are getting longer and the spring bulbs are in full bloom. After a long, bleak winter, the temptation is to devote all your gardening energy to the production of flowers. By all means plant the spring flowers, but don't forget to include a good foundation of foliage to add character to the garden.

Take the peony, for example. Within a month or so, each peony will be laden with blooms so heavy the plants can barely support them. But in the very early days of spring the peony is far more delicate and mysterious, as curled red fronds push their way above the ground. Hostas, too, are especially graceful when their leaves unfurl in pristine glory, while ferns look impossibly fragile as they first emerge. Maple trees that will become dense and heavy with foliage by midsummer start the spring with early bursts of red, lime green, and inconspicuous but interesting flowers.

The big bulbs steal the show, but take time to inspect the winter aconite (*Eranthis hyemalis*, syn. *Eranthis cilicia*), with its tiny petticoat of foliage, and the delicate leaves of the windflower (*Anemone blanda*). Before the tall, stately tulips dominate the garden, earlier tulip varieties hug the ground and show off their colorful leaves. 'Heart's Delight', a Kaufmanniana type tulip, is one of the first to bloom, with mottled leaves to offset its flowers. Next come the Greigii tulips, such as the scarlet 'Red Riding Hood' with its brown and purple leaves. New tulips are introduced each year—since they will need

ABOVE: ***The bright white margins of* Hosta albo-marginata *add a cheerful note to this shady planting. Among the hundreds of hostas available today are those with solid medium green, dark green, chartreuse, yellow, blue, or blue-green leaves. They may have white, yellow, green, or blue-green margins or they may be streaked or splashed with white, yellow, or green, or with a combination of these colors.***

LEFT: ***If you picture ferns as tall, dark, and boring, Japanese painted fern (*Athyrium goeringianum *'Pictum', syn.* A. nipponicum *'Pictum') will broaden your outlook. Growing to only 12–18 inches (30–45cm) tall, with silvery fronds touched with burgundy and green, this is a fern for connoisseurs.***

to be replaced periodically, look for those that have the added benefit of interesting foliage.

Later in the season the leaves of violets (*Viola* spp.) may look a little chewed, but in early spring the rounded or heart-shaped leaves form neat little mounds that look great even when the plants aren't in flower. Pasque flower (*Pusillata vulgaris*) emerges early in the season looking like some fuzzy alien life form. After the brightly colored flowers fade, the seedheads will give pasque flowers another few weeks of interest. Plant them in a sunny spot where they won't be disturbed—pasque flowers don't like to be moved around.

The fuzzy buds of magnolia, velvety pussywillow, and fragrant witchhazel are always welcome in the spring. The Mohawk viburnum (*Viburnum* x *burkwoodii* 'Mohawk') is a plant for all seasons, starting out with glossy leaves and dark red flower buds, followed by fragrant flowers and many months of attractive foliage on a fairly compact shrub. Azaleas and rhododendrons are beautiful in leaf, bud, and bloom, but be sure to plant them in the kind of place they love—sheltered under trees, in moist, acidic soil with lots of organic matter.

Some cultivars of Japanese quince (*Chaenomeles speciosa*) have beautiful, glossy foliage and attractive flowers, but beware of the thorns. Japanese barberry *(Berberis thunbergii* 'Crimson Pygmy') is another thorny but attractive shrub; it is also one of the first shrubs to leaf out in spring.

At the opposite end of the spectrum, spring is the best time to appreciate the lacy foliage of bleeding heart (*Dicentra* spp.), and the equally lacy emerging foliage of poppies (*Papaver* spp.) and love-in-a-mist (*Nigella damascena*). Other spring plants with attractive foliage include epimedium (*Epimedium* spp.) and Bethlehem sage (*Pulmonaria* spp.). This is also the best time to see many wildflowers, including bloodroot (*Sanguinaria canadensis*), jack-in-the-pulpit (*Arisaema triphyllum*), mayapple (*Podophyllum peltatum*), and trillium (*Trillium grandiflorum*), many of which have foliage as attractive as their flowers.

BELOW: ***Bring the brilliant colors of autumn to the garden all season long with this inspired planting of Japanese barberry (*****Berberis thunbergii*****) cultivars 'Golden Ring' and 'Aurea'. While Japanese barberry is wonderfully ornamental and easy to grow, the thorny branches can be nasty. Plant them a safe distance from children and summer-bare legs.***

A SHADED GARDEN IN SPRING

First of all, a word about what this garden is not: it is not a traditional shade garden. It is easy to plan a shady garden with hostas and ferns, especially when the accent is on foliage. I can always find a place for a few more hostas, but this plan for a shaded spring garden puts more emphasis on smaller-leaved plants that do well in shade, such as pulmonaria and lamium. Epimedium is a plant that does well in dry shade, but I did not include the genus because most of the plants in this plan will do better in a fairly moist shade.

It is easy to find plans for small, shady gardens, but it is more difficult to tackle the landscaping of a home on a shaded lot. This plan includes several trees with ornamental foliage, but don't let that scare you. Use the plan as a starting point, working with existing plants in your landscape. The island bed features a variety of groundcovers that can be planted in tree circles under trees in your yard instead of duplicating the plan. Use the plant list and plant combinations as experiments with shade-loving alternatives to traditional foundation plants.

The lacy-leaved red Japanese maple in the plan can be substituted by any number of fine cultivars. I have placed it in a protected corner since Japanese maples are not famous for their endurance in extreme weather. The redbud has the combined benefit of attractive, heart-shaped foliage and beautiful spring flowers that emerge before the leaves. There are many alternatives to the eastern redbud, including 'Royal White' (white-flowering), 'Forest Pansy' (a purple-leaved cultivar), the smaller Chinese redbud which is recommended for the South (*Cercis chinensis*), and other species that are ornamental but generally less hardy.

I have included a cultivar of dwarf fothergilla called 'Blue Mist' for its attractive blue foliage in spring and summer. Oregon grapeholly does well in shade and with a little protection—in exposed areas the foliage has a tendency to brown, but it is worth the extra care for the benefit of its unique foliage, fruit, and flowers. Hemlocks also perform better with shade and shelter, although I have occasionally seen hemlocks thriving in sun. All hemlocks look soft and feathery compared to the stiff needles and formal appearance of spruce, but 'Gentsch White' has the added highlight of white tipped branches.

'Elizabeth' is not your everyday magnolia; this yellow-flowering form was the result of a cross between the cucumbertree magnolia and the Yulan magnolia. The 'Schwedler' maple, a Norway maple cultivar included for its purply-red spring foliage, has been around for a hundred years and is easy to find.

In addition to several groundcovers with interesting foliage, the accompanying plan includes rodgersia, an outstanding, moisture-loving foliage plant that is often used around ponds, a spiky form of astilbe, and a peony that will grab attention when it flowers in mid- to late spring. It is fascinating to watch the red shoots of peonies unfurl in early spring, and the neat mounds of foliage look attractive during the summer and often into the fall. Heartleaf brunnera is always beautiful in flower, but the variegated form in this plan extends the season of interest. The same holds true for the silvery leaves of 'Sylvetta', a Korean violet that looks great peeking out from under other plants.

PLANT LIST

SUGGESTED QUANTITIES ARE NOTED AFTER EACH PLANT NAME.

1. *Acer palmatum* var. *distichum* 'Red Filigree Lace' (Japanese maple)—1
2. *Tsuga canadensis* 'Gentsch White' (hemlock)—6
3. *Fothergilla gardenii* 'Blue Mist' (dwarf fothergilla)—2
4. *Cercis canadensis* (redbud)—1
5. *Acer platanoides* 'Schwedler' ('Schwedler' Norway maple)—1
6. *Picea pungens* 'Thomsen' ('Thomsen' blue spruce)—1
7. *Cornus controversa* 'Variegata' (variegated giant dogwood)—1
8. *Magnolia* × 'Elizabeth' (hybrid magnolia 'Elizabeth')—1

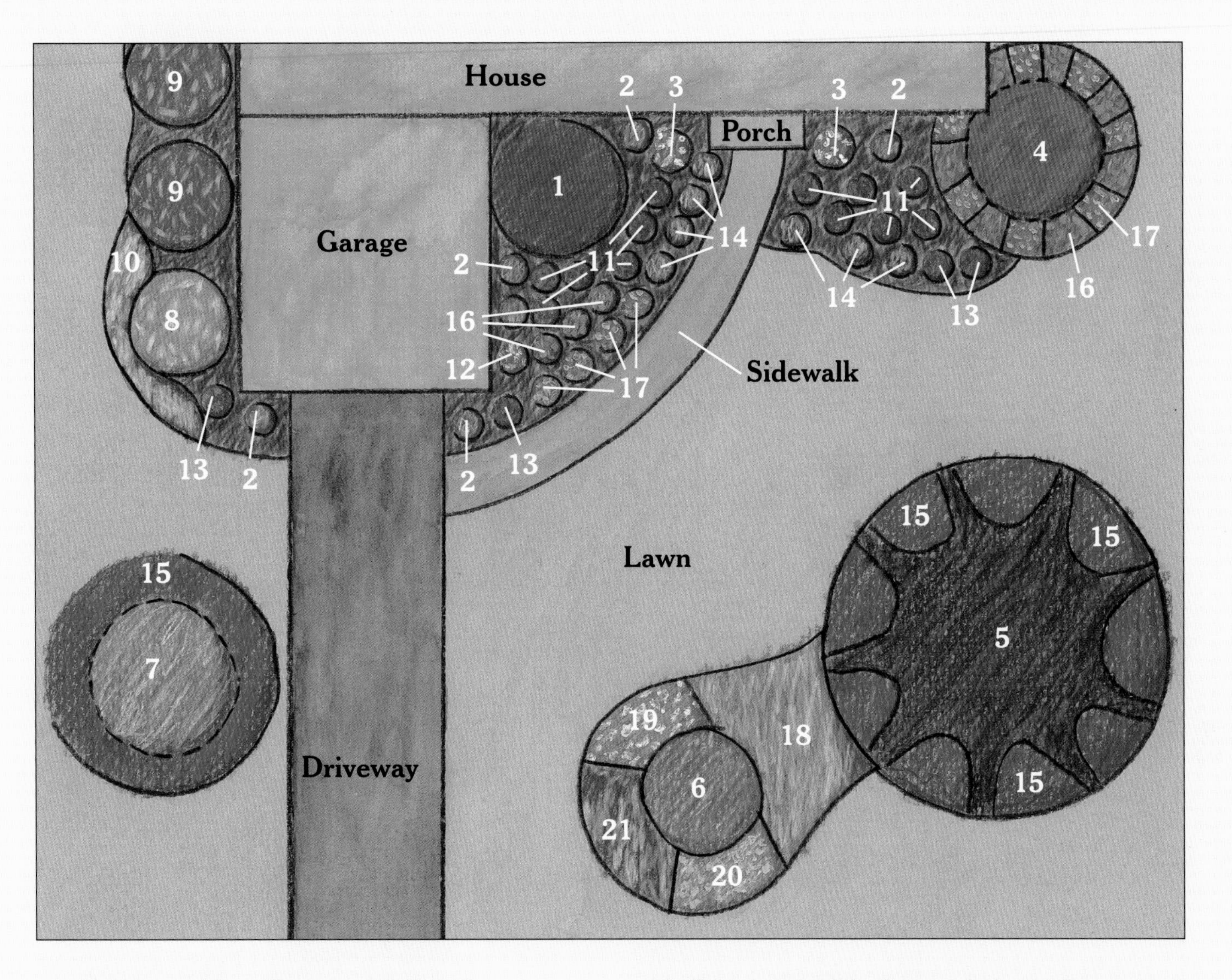

9. *Mahonia aquifolium* (Oregon grapeholly)—2

10. *Pulmonaria* × 'Excalibur' (lungwort)—6

11. *Astilbe taquetti* 'Superba' (autumn astilbe)—12

12. *Rodgersia pinnata* 'Superba' (rodgersia)—2

13. *Paeonia* × 'Lake of Silver' (hybrid peony)—4

14. *Viola koreana* 'Sylvetta' (violet)—7

15. *Pachysandra terminalis* 'Green Sheen' (Japanese spurge)—12

16. *Pulmonaria longifolia* 'Bertram Anderson' (lungwort)—6

17. *Lamium maculatum* 'Pink Pewter' (dead nettle)—8

18. *Brunnera macrophylla* 'Variegata' (syn. *Anchusa myosotidiflora*) (heartleaf brunnera; variegated forget-me-not)—12

19. *Lamium maculatum* 'White Nancy' (dead nettle)—6

20. *Pulmonaria* × 'Victorian Brooch' (lungwort)—6

21. *Ajuga reptans* 'Burgundy Glow' (bugleweed)—6

Great Groundcovers

ABOVE: ***A profusion of ivy (*****Hedera helix*****) covers the ground around a small pool. Ivy can be somewhat tender in northern climes, so give it a protected spot.***

The term "groundcover" usually refers to a perennial plant that will spread quickly enough to cover the ground in a few seasons and densely enough to crowd out weeds. When you get right down to it, grass is one of the best groundcovers of all. Under ideal situations, groundcovers save a gardener lots of time and effort. A planting bed with a nice, clean spaded edge, a little mulch, and a mass of groundcover to green up the bare spots adds a polished touch to any landscape.

The most popular groundcovers vary from region to region, but certainly myrtle (*Vinca* spp., also called periwinkle) is one of the most common. Annual vinca (*Vinca major*) is a good substitute for impatiens in sunny spots, since it flowers from early spring to late autumn, becomes a nice, bushy mound that discourages weeds, and has attractive flowers and glossy, green leaves. The perennial form of vinca (*Vinca minor*) is a popular groundcover for sunny spots. It takes a season or two to become established, and in some areas has recently fallen prey to a variety of blights, but under ideal circumstances it can be breathtaking. The cultivars 'Ralph Shugert' and 'Sterling Silver' are touched with a silvery variegation that I prefer to the solid green foliage.

Japanese spurge (*Pachysandra terminalis*) is a good groundcover for shady areas. Some gardeners treat it with disdain, but I think pachysandra is very attractive when planted under trees and shrubs. It doesn't always mix well with perennials, but it makes a solid carpet of green, and the foliage is clean and glossy with finely toothed edges. Two popular cultivars are 'Silver Edge', a variegated form, and 'Green Carpet', which has a good, deep green color.

To fill in a space or slope quickly, some people use crown vetch (*Coronilla varia*). The cultivar 'Penngift' is said to be neater than the species, but generally I would not recommend crown vetch because it can so easily spread beyond control. It tends to get a little straggly looking, too.

Purpleleaf wintercreeper (*Euonymus fortunei* 'Coloratus') is also used to cover slopes or large beds, and I prefer this versatile groundcover. The foliage is very attractive, especially in the autumn, and it quickly crowds out any weeds. The only drawback is that it does need occasional trimming to keep it looking neat.

Sweet woodruff (*Galium odoratum*) is a delicate-looking plant that makes quite an effective groundcover on a small scale. The tiny flowers are fairly insignificant, and the foliage has been described as smelling like hay. Sweet woodruff is sometimes used to make a kind of May wine. Yellow archangel (formerly *Lamiastrum galeobdolon*, now *Lamium galeobdolon*) is a quickly spreading perennial that works well as a groundcover in woodland gardens. Several cultivars of dead nettle (*Lamium maculatum*) will add interest to shady gardens, although they don't form as dense a mat as a plant like pachysandra. Look for 'White Nancy', 'Beacon Silver', 'Pink Pewter', 'Sterling Silver', and 'Shell Pink' and try them on a small scale between hostas or under a tree. Ivy (*Hedera helix*) is often used as a groundcover, but unless it is in a sheltered spot, it may not survive a tough winter.

Groundcovers suitable for sunnier gardens include creeping thyme, a variety of sedums including 'Dragon's Blood', prostrate spruce and low, spreading junipers, creeping speedwell (*Veronica* spp.), and pink tickseed (*Coreopsis rosea*).

These plants can solve a variety of landscape problems, and will add beauty to your garden with lovely, long-lasting foliage.

ABOVE: ***Japanese spurge (*****Pachysandra terminalis*****) forms a dense groundcover in shady areas, and its glossy foliage doesn't need flowers to make it look good. The variegated 'Silver Edge' makes a bright accent planted in a tree circle around the base of a small tree and does not compete with the tree's roots as much as a lawn would.***
BELOW: ***In ideal conditions, periwinkle (*****Vinca minor*****) will spread enough under trees or shrubs to crowd out weeds in semishady areas. It takes a season or two to become established and may require weeding at first, but the delicate leaves and tiny blue flowers are well worth that small effort.***

HOSTAS AND FERNS

No foliage garden would be complete without a selection of hostas and ferns. They are easy to grow and care for; all they need is a spot with a little shade and, especially for the ferns, some even moisture. The uninitiated may just see hostas as mounds of green or variegated green and white, while if they think of ferns at all it is likely as filler in a flower arrangement or in a dark corner of the yard. For those who treasure interesting foliage, though, hostas and ferns are rich with landscaping possibilities.

FERNS FOR ROCK GARDENS, GROUNDCOVER, OR EDGING

Asplenium platyneuron (ebony spleenwort)

Athyrium goeringianum, syn. *A. niponicum* var. *pictum* (Japanese painted fern)

Ceterach officinarum, syn. *Asplenium ceterach* (rusty-back fern)

Cheilanthes lanosa (hairy-lip fern)

Gymnocarpium dryopteris (oak fern)

Phegopteris connectilis, syn. *Thelypteris phegopteris* (beech fern)

Polystichum tsus-simense (Korean rock fern)

HOSTAS FOR ROCK GARDENS, GROUNDCOVER, OR EDGING

Hosta 'Chartreuse Wiggles'

Hosta 'Cheesecake'

Hosta 'Crown Jewel'

Hosta 'Golden Tiara'

Hosta 'Kabitan'

Hosta 'Lights Up'

Hosta 'Stiletto'

MID-SIZE, INTERESTING, AND DEPENDABLE FERNS

Adiantum pedatum (maidenhair fern)

Phytillis scolopendrium (hart's tongue fern)

Polystichum acrostichoides (Christmas fern)

Polystichum munitum (sword fern)

TOP: ***While most ferns are identified by their foliage, cinnamon fern (*****Osmunda cinnamomea*****) is easy to spot by the rich, cinnamon-colored fertile fronds that make it a standout in the shade garden.***

CENTER: ***Where color is the primary attraction in traditional, sunny gardens, the subtle features of a foliage garden focus more on combinations of form and texture. The small leaves of barrenwort (*****Epimedium*** ***spp.) sprawl in fragile-looking layers like elongated hearts, while the waving fronds of sword fern (*****Polystichum munitum*****) spread gracefully in the dappled shade.***

BOTTOM: ***Rich moist soil and a bit of shade is about all that is needed for ostrich fern (*****Matteuccia struthiopteris*****) to thrive. The towering 5-foot (1.5m) clumps look great at the back of a shady border or used to disguise a wall or shed.***

Mid-Size, Interesting, and Dependable Hostas

Hosta 'Bold Ruffles'
Hosta 'Francee'
Hosta 'Frances Williams'
Hosta 'Inniswood'
Hosta 'Love Pat'
Hosta 'Royal Standard'
Hosta 'Wide Brim'
Hosta montana 'Aureomarginata'
Hosta plantaginea 'Aphrodite'
Hosta tokudama 'Aureonebulosa'

Ferns with Large, Bold Foliage

Dryopteris goldiana (Goldie's wood fern)
Dryopteris erythrosora (autumn fern)
Matteuccia struthiopteris (ostrich fern)
Osmunda cinamomea (cinnamon fern)
Osmunda regalis (royal fern)

Hostas with Large, Bold Foliage

Hosta 'Big Daddy'
Hosta 'Blue Angel'
Hosta 'Blue Mammoth'
Hosta 'Great Expectations'
Hosta 'Green Fountain'
Hosta 'Regal Splendor'
Hosta 'Sum and Substance'
Hosta fluctuans 'Sagae' (formerly *Hosta fluctuans* 'Variegated')
Hosta sieboldiana 'Elegans'

ABOVE: ***If you think of foliage as green, try to count the colors in this wonderfully integrated island bed. Bright green, forest green, light green, chartreuse, soft yellow, cream, creamy green, blue, blue green—and that's just a start! Featured plants include*** **Hosta sieboldiana** ***'Elegans', golden queen-of-the-meadow (*****Filipendula ulmaria** ***'Aurea'), and Welsh poppy (*****Meconopsis cambrica*****).***

ABOVE: ***Large, thickly textured, blue hosta leaves are edged with yellow-green margins that highlight the color of the feathery ferns. Feathery, cutleaf Japanese maple leaves in a rich burgundy-bronze pull the whole picture together.***
RIGHT: ***It is no wonder that*** Hosta ***'Francee' is consistently a favorite with hosta experts and home gardeners alike. It works equally well in mixed hosta shade beds or as a specimen, as in this artistic tableau.***

Chapter 3

Stars of Summer

It's easy to think of flowers as the stars of summer because they are so bright and colorful. Bedding plants in hot colors are packed into every yard, shopping mall, and commercial building in sight. Impatiens and begonias abound. Bright, bountiful . . . boring? Well, not always, but sometimes an interesting foliage planting seems almost a relief, especially when it is baking hot outside.

*'Checquers' lamium (*Lamium maculatum *'Chequers') brightens shady areas with its cool silver variegation and small, amethyst-colored flowers. This trouble-free groundcover will fill in quickly in cooler climates; in the South the plants may suffer somewhat from the heat and need to be replaced every few years.*

Summer is a stressful time for plants, because even those that like heat don't always like the conditions that go with it—drought in some areas and humidity in others. Ornamental grasses really come into their own in late summer, just as a lot of plants are starting to fade. Late-blooming grasses such as Japanese silver grass (*Miscanthus* spp.) have wonderful plumes that add interest to the plant, but it lookes great even when not in "flower." In extremely hot climates, even tough ornamental grasses may need to be situated in some shade, but generally Japanese silver grass performs best in full sun.

Many plants with silver, gray, or white foliage are able to withstand extremes of heat and drought. Wormwood (*Artemisia* spp.) is readily available and comes in many forms, from the relatively neat 'Silvermound' to the rapidly spreading 'Silver King' and the lacy 'Powis Castle'. Sage and euphorbia are also available in a variety of forms, most of which are both attractive and able to withstand a sizzling summer. Snow-in-summer (*Cerastium tomentosum*) grows like a groundcover and is covered with white flowers in late spring and early summer. Even after the flowers are spent, the low mats of silvery foliage look attractive, although they are not quite dense enough to crowd out weeds. Lamb's ear (*Stachys byzantina*) is velvety to the touch, with foliage so distinctive that many gardeners plant only nonflowering varieties. The blue-gray foliage of carnations and pinks is an indication that they will also perform well in summer's heat.

It can also be visually cooling to add some dark, purplish plants to the summer landscape. Purpleleaf plums, sand cherries, 'Rosybloom' crabapples, 'Crimson Pygmy' barberry, purple smoketree, and 'Crimson King' maples are just a few of the darker-leaved plants to consider. Perennials with red or burgundy foliage are also a refreshing sight in summer, providing a foil for blue-, silver-, or gray-leaved plants. For a moist spot, you can hardly beat *Rodgersia pinnata* 'Superba'—its large leaves are a deep, bronze-purple that make just about any accompanying plant look even better. Another favorite in the bronze-to-purple range is *Heuchera micrantha* 'Palace Purple', a form of coral bells with foliage that far outshines its flowers. Bugleweed (*Ajuga* spp.) is available in a variety of species and cultivars that have foliage colors ranging from burgundy to pink to purple to bronze to silver, and every variegation in between. Bugleweed is something you either love or hate—it is extremely invasive, although a few cultivars are less so, but it does have attractive foliage and spring flowers, and it is an effective groundcover.

Flowers may hold the frontline in most summer gardens, but a solid backbone of interesting foliage can keep the garden looking great when the flowers have passed their prime.

LEFT: ***The deep reddish purple leaves of 'Crimson Pygmy' barberry (*****Berberis thunbergii*** ***'Crimson Pygmy') offer soothing tones in the summer garden. This compact shrub makes an excellent low hedge, or may be mixed with taller shrubs. It is also at home as a specimen in a rock garden.***

ABOVE: *Some gardeners feel that the tall, unspectacular flowers of lamb's ears (*Stachys *spp.) detract from the velvety foliage that makes this perennial so popular. As shown here, though, the flowers make a perfect foil for companion plants hybrid Hungarian speedwell (*Veronica teucrium *'True Blue') and cranesbill geranium (*Geranium × oxonianum *'Claridge Druce'). Gardeners seeking to avoid flowers may select the cultivar 'Silver Carpet', but be warned that its spread can be prolific.*

A GARDEN OF GOLD AND GREEN

Green and gold were the school colors of Elk Grove High School, where I walked the halls in the days of yore, so I look on this combination with a certain affection. Nature seems to enjoy the combination, too, since it is so common both in the pairing of flower and leaf and in variegated form on leaves or needles. Green is a gentle, relaxing color—easy on the eyes. Bright yellow and gold wake us up with a jolt—this mix of soothing and sassy keeps us on our toes.

Hostas highlight this garden plan, simply because they are easy to find, easy to use, and easy to grow. They are not always cheap, but feel free to substitute similar but less expensive varieties if they are better suited to your landscape budget. One benefit of hostas, as opposed to other perennials, some of which seem to think they are annuals, is that they are pretty hard to kill. Deer might munch them, rabbits might crunch them, but still they come back. Slugs might turn the leaves to lace, an April frost might turn the foliage brown, but still the new shoots push up and out. Plant them in part shade, in soil that stays fairly moist (add compost before planting to help the soil retain water, and mulch after planting), and you can hardly go wrong.

Lady's mantle is likewise easy to grow, and the foliage is highly photogenic, especially when morning dew settles in the cupped leaves. In good soil it will spread, but not unmanageably. The chartreuse flowers are attractive but not overwhelming—they add interest without taking away from the appeal of the foliage. Cranesbill geranium is a good perennial for edging beds; a tendency to sprawl is easily forgiven when the vivid flowers bloom and again in autumn when the foliage turns a mix of brilliant colors. Hakone grass, unlike many ornamental grasses, performs better in shade than in sun and even a small planting will catch the eye.

The variegated leaves of 'Brise d'Anjou' Jacob's ladder will continue to highlight the garden long after the flowers have faded. *Chrysanthemum pacificum* will come as a surprise to gardeners who have not tried it—far from the bold and brassy chrysanthemums that are autumn standards, this low-growing perennial has silver-edged leaves and tiny masses of yellow flowers that are a secondary attraction. Within a few years, the neat foliage will spread into a textured swale of groundcover.

The featured trees are not the hardiest cultivars, but they are certainly the brightest.

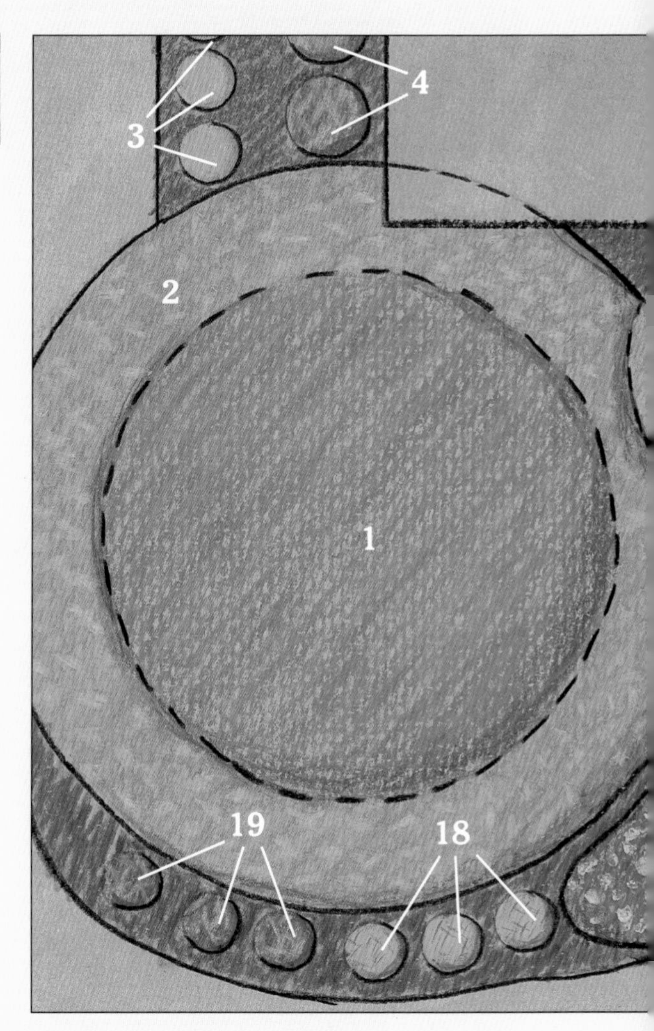

'Sunburst' honeylocust is smaller and less vigorous than the common 'Skyline' honeylocust, but it is a perfect size for a small yard. The golden full moon maple has leaves like hands with fingers splayed, a light green washed with gold. All of the plants in this garden will perform well with part shade, part sun, and soil that is moist but well-drained. Planting the golden full moon maple near the house

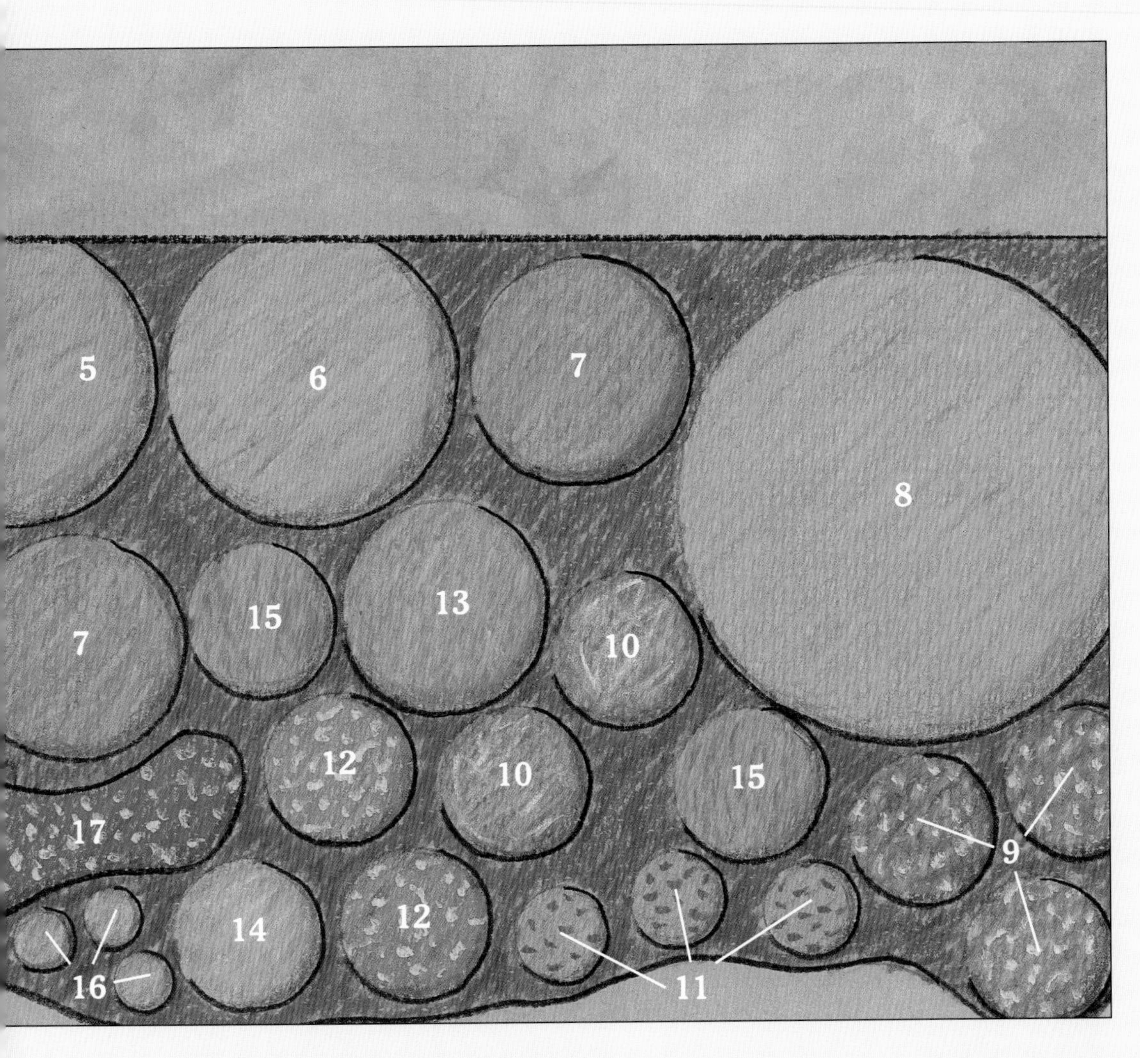

will provide protection —it is relatively hardy but a little caution never hurt.

Cover bare spots in the newly planted garden with about 3 inches (7cm) of mulch — no more than that—and be careful not to let the mulch mound up near the base of the plants or trees. Instead, hollow out a well around the base of each plant to allow water to drain near the roots.

PLANT LIST

SUGGESTED QUANTITIES ARE NOTED AFTER EACH PLANT NAME.

1. *Gleditsia triacanthos* var. *inermis* 'Sunburst' ('Sunburst' thornless honeylocust)—1
2. *Lysimacia nummularia* (creeping Jenny, moneywort)—6
3. *Hosta* × 'Little Aurora' (hosta)—3
4. *Hosta* × 'Golden Tiara' (hosta)—3
5. *Hosta* × 'Solar Flare' (hosta)—1
6. *Hosta* × 'Sum and Substance' (hosta)—1
7. *Hosta* × 'Sunshine Glory' (hosta)—2
8. *Acer japonicum* 'Aureum' (syn. *Acer shirasawanum* 'Aureum') (golden full moon maple)—1
9. *Alchemilla mollis* (lady's mantle)—3
10. *Polemonium caeruleum* 'Brise d'Anjou' (variegated Jacob's ladder)—2
11. *Geranium* × 'Ann Folkard' (cranesbill geranium)—3
12. *Corydalis lutea* (yellow fumitory)—2
13. *Hosta* × 'Sun Power' (hosta)—1
14. *Hakonechloa macra* 'Aureola' (hakone grass)—1
15. *Hosta* × 'Gold Standard' (hosta)—2
16. *Hosta* × 'Little Sunspot' (hosta)—3
17. *Chrysanthemum pacificum* (syn. *Dendranthema pacificum*) (groundcover chrysanthemum)—4
18. *Hosta* × 'Kabitan' (hosta)—3
19. *Hosta* × 'Stiletto' (hosta)—3

DROUGHT-TOLERANT PLANTS

Hot, dry summers combined with water restrictions make drought-tolerant plants look mighty attractive. Many drought-resistant plants have the added benefit of beautiful foliage. This list includes many kinds of plants—trees, shrubs, and perennials—but not all will be hardy in every area. Below is a general guide to drought-tolerant plants—before making selections check to be sure that you have chosen wisely for the planting conditions in your garden.

TREES

Acacia spp. (acacia)
Cedrus spp. (cedar)
Celtis spp. (hackberry)
Cercis canadensis (redbud)
Cupressus glabra (Arizona cypress)
Gymnocladus dioica (Kentucky coffeetree)
Koelreuteria paniculata (golden raintree)
Pinus spp. (pine)
Prunus tomentosa (Nanking cherry)
Quercus spp. (oak)
Robinia spp. (locust)
Rhus spp. (sumac)
Tamarix spp. (tamarisk)
Tilia spp. (linden)

SHRUBS

Chaenomeles spp. (flowering quince)
Cotoneaster spp. (cotoneaster)
Eleaganus spp. (olive)
Hypericum spp. (St. John's wort)
Juniperus spp. (juniper)
Myrtus spp. (myrtle)
Potentilla fruticosa (potentilla)
Rosa foetida (Austrian copper rose)
Rosa rubrifolia (red-leaved rose)
Teucricum spp. (germander)

LEFT: ***Oaks are well-loved for their strength and their distinctive branching, but many are also tolerant of drought situations. The Oregon white oak*** **(Quercus garryana)** ***shown here can be found growing along the West Coast from British Columbia down through California.***

RIGHT: ***Creeping juniper (*****Juniperus horizontalis*****) happily withstands scorching sun and a scarcity of water. This low-growing evergreen is perfect for a rock garden or for any well-drained site.***

PERENNIALS

Agave spp. (agave)
Amorpha canescens (false indigo)
Artemisia spp. (wormwood)
Baptisia australis (indigo)
Centranthus ruber (red valerian)
Coreopsis spp. (tickseed)
Echinops spp. (globe thistle)
Gaillardia spp. (blanket flower)
Iris spp. (iris)
Lavandula spp. (lavender)
Liatris spp. (gayfeather)
Linum spp. (flax)
Perovskia atriplicifolia (Russian sage)
Phormium tenax (New Zealand flax)
Rosmarinus spp. (rosemary)
Yucca spp. (Adam's needle)

RIGHT: ***'Powis Castle' artemisia (*****Artemisia × 'Powis Castle'*****) grows as a spreading shrub, and may reach 4 feet (1.2m) in height. Like many silver-leaved plants, artemisia is native to dry climates and needs to be watered only sparingly.***

ORNAMENTAL GRASSES AND BAMBOOS

How times have changed. Not all that long ago gardeners looked on grasses with disdain. They were too tall, too messy, too much like weeds and—worst of all—they didn't have flowers. One clear-sighted firm of landscape architects did a lot to change our view of grasses, developing a style of landscape design that involved bold sweeps of ornamental grasses and perennials, primarily *Rudbeckia fulgida* var. *sullivanti* 'Goldsturm' and *Hylotelephium* x 'Autumn Joy' (formerly *Sedum* x 'Autumn Joy').

The grasses we see in gardens today originated not in lawns but across prairies, in bogs, and along coastlines. They vary considerably in their soil and site requirements—not all, as some seem to think, can be planted anywhere it's sunny and dry. Many ornamental grasses are so neat and compact it's hard to believe they could have ever been considered weedy. Others are massive and spread into tall, thick clumps. And while they might not be decorated with bright baubles of flowers, they do have wonderfully textured seed and flowerheads that are a blessed relief to the jaded gardener.

Popular grasses include species of *Miscanthus* (Japanese silver grass), *Molina* (purple moor grass), *Festuca* (blue fescue), *Pennisetum* (fountain grass), *Helictotrichon* (blue oat grass), *Calamagrostis* (feather reed grass), *Carex* (sedge), *Deschampsia* (tufted hair grass), *Panicum* (switch grass), and *Phalaris* (ribbon grass). Variegated hakone grass (*Hakonechloa macra*) is beautiful for a shady spot, while a cultivar of switch grass (*Panicum virgatum* 'Rehbraun', syn. 'Haense Herms' and 'Rotstrahlbusch') goes through two stages of autumn color—in July and again in October.

Bamboos seem to be either unknown and untried, or tried and found invasive. Few gardeners who have seen bamboo growing would deny its architectural and ornamental value. The problem is that many types of bamboo are fairly uncontrollable and must be ruled out for small lots. On the other hand, some are reasonably easy to control, and may have other virtues to recommend them. Many newer introductions are extremely ornamental, and some species are also said to be delicious to eat. Environmentalists have also found that its invasiveness can sometimes be a plus, especially when a site requires erosion control or a windbreak.

Bamboo is long-lived, pest resistant, and generally prefers a moist site; it can be very susceptible to cold weather, though. Two recommended forms are both hardy and restrained—umbrella bamboo (*Fargesia murielae*) and fountain bamboo (*Fargesia nitida*). Blue bamboo (*Phyllostachys nigra* 'Henon') is another interesting type of bamboo, though its extreme height restricts its usefulness. At the other end of the spectrum is a groundcover bamboo, *Pleioblastus viridi-striata*, that is very hardy and has bright yellow foliage. One shade-loving bamboo, *Sasa veitchii*, has a variegated appearance, although it is invasive.

Be adventurous—if you haven't found a spot for grasses or bamboos in your garden, first ensure that you have selected a hardy species that will not get out of hand, then take that first step into a new world of garden plants.

OPPOSITE: ***The neat lines of this secluded corner will be attractive in all seasons. The tall, leafy spikes of lilies, about to bloom behind the bench, will add summer interest; graceful sprays of ornamental grass will be effective even in winter.*** RIGHT: ***Ribbon grass*** **(Phalaris arundinacea *var.* picta*)* *creates a fountain of leaves beside a pond.***

A GARDEN OF SILVER AND WHITE

Summer: shimmering heat, flowers blazing in orange, yellow, and red, grass baked to a tawny blonde. In the middle of that heat, picture a garden in silver, white, and gray against a backdrop of cool green. As it happens, nature is on the gardener's side in this endeavor, since many silver, gray, and white plants have Mediterranean origins. Hot sun reflecting on pale rocks or white sidewalks may signal the end to many perennials, but the plants included in this garden plan should prevail against the withering heat. Plants that are able to withstand heat and drought still need time to become established, though, and the best way to ensure their survival is to plant them long before or after the heat of midday and to keep them well-watered (not flooded) for several weeks at least.

Situate this island bed either where it can be observed while you are sprawled in a hammock, lounging on the deck, or out in front to break up an expanse of lawn. This garden will sprawl and ramble, instead of neatly staying put. Children (grownups, too) will want to touch the woolly leaves of silver sage, stroke the velvety lamb's ears, and run their fingers through the silvery fronds of switch grass. Even in its first year, this garden will be a surprise, starting out with small plants that by late summer will already be experiencing growth spurts. In its second year, the butterfly bush should swarm with living colors and tiny, flapping wings while the bees swarm around the white spikes of gayfeather. The weeping pear may need training at first to keep its trunk from taking on a corkscrew shape, but as it grows this little tree will become a focal point of the garden. The cultivar I have featured, 'Silver Frost', has a better chance of surviving the risks of fire blight unscathed than a weeping willowleaf pear that does not have a cultivar ("cultivated variety") name.

Rabbits and groundhogs love cottage pinks, but they are doing you a favor when they munch on spent flowerheads. Cottage pinks that have been sheared, whether by teeth or by shears, usually come back with a second flush of flowers that may surpass the first. Deadhead the coneflowers if you want another, smaller, period of bloom. White-flowering butterfly bush does tend to look rather worse for wear when the white flowers eventually turn brown. Clip off the dead flowerheads and the reward will often be a new flush of flowers. Snow-in-summer may not look like much when you plant it, but don't pass it up based on the appearance of a few tiny leaves in a 3-inch (7cm) pot. One plant will creep into a space one foot square or more within a year or two, and when it bursts into bloom don't be surprised if people knock on your door to inquire what plant it might be.

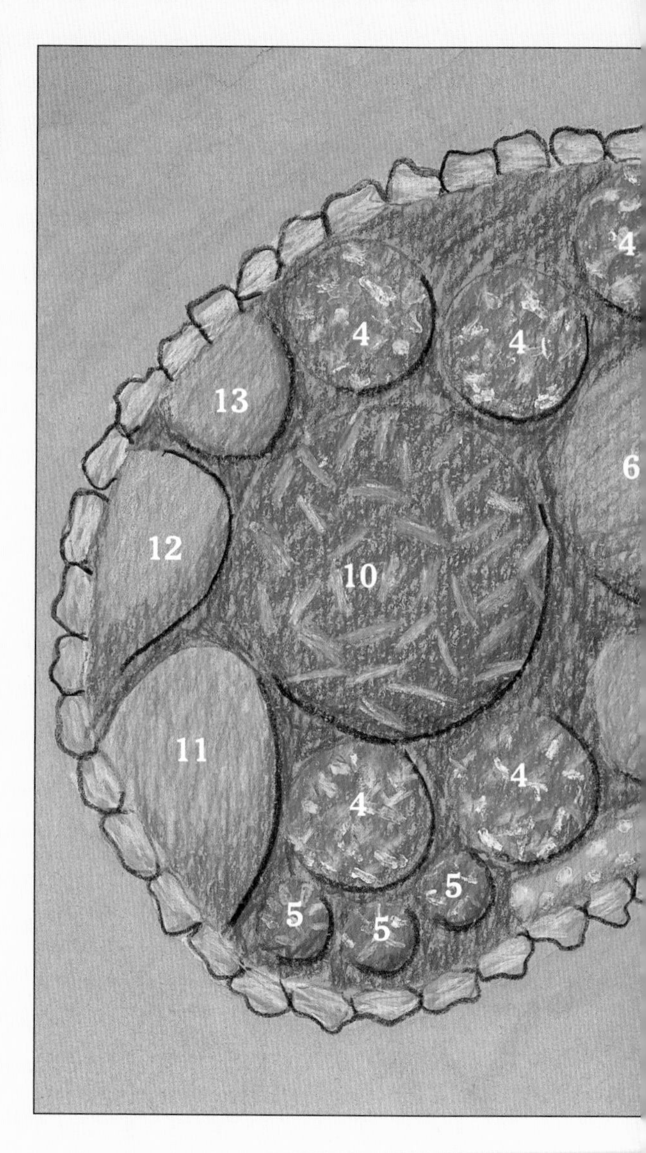

After this garden has had a year or two to become established, you may suddenly have enough plants to replicate the whole design over again in someone else's yard. In good soil, lamb's ears can multiply prolifically, but neighbors, schools, and churches are almost always happy to take the extras off your hands. Cut back the various forms of artemisia periodically to keep the plants

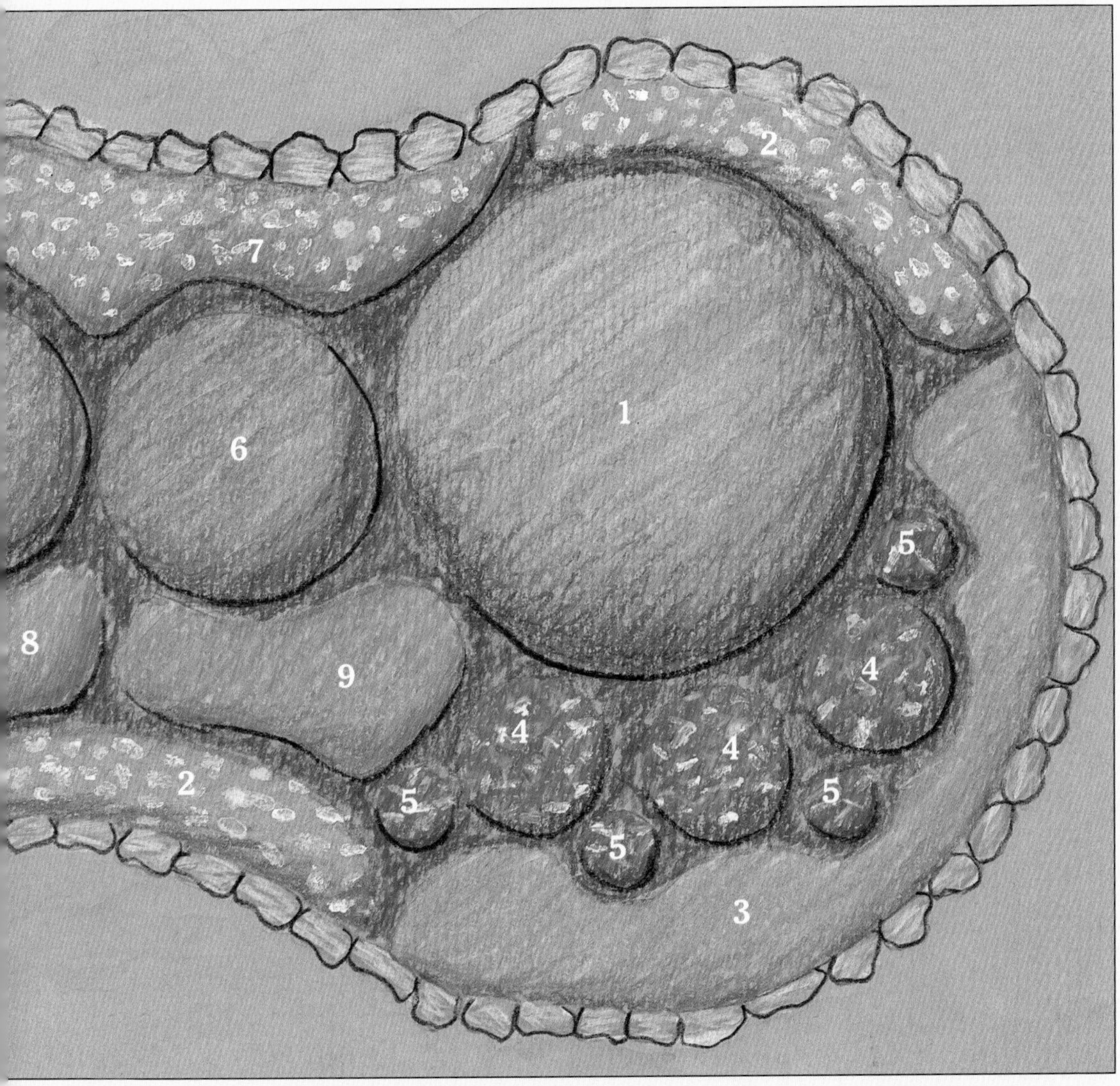

PLANT LIST

SUGGESTED QUANTITIES ARE NOTED AFTER EACH PLANT NAME.

1. *Pyrus salicifolia* 'Silver Frost' (weeping willowleaf pear)—1
2. *Cerastium tomentosum* 'Silver Carpet' (snow-in-summer)—10
3. *Stachys byzantina* (syn. *Stachys olympica*) 'Silver Carpet' (lamb's ears)—6
4. *Echinacea purpurea* 'Alba' (white coneflower)—8
5. *Liatris scariosa* var. *alba* 'Whitespire' (gayfeather)—7
6. *Panicum virgatum* 'Heavy Metal' (switch grass)—2
7. *Dianthus plumarius* 'It Saul White' (cottage pinks)—4
8. *Artemisia absinthium* 'Lambrook Silver' (wormwood, artemisia)—3
9. *Artemisia* × 'Powis Castle' (wormwood hybrid)—3
10. *Buddleia davidii* 'White Ball' (butterfly bush)—1
11. *Artemisia stelleriana* 'Silver Brocade' (beach wormwood)—2
12. *Artemisia schmidtiana* 'Silver Mound'(silvermound artemisia)—3
13. *Salvia argentea* (silver sage)—4

from getting too messy, although a certain amount of silvery sprawl keeps the garden looking lush.

As an incentive to perform the boring job of deadheading, many of the plants in this garden are ideal specimens for drying—whether for foliage or flowers. Why pay a fortune for dried flower arrangements when you can grow your own?

Mulch the empty spaces between the little plants you install, and in a year or two you will barely recognize the island bed. Once established, these plants will require very little maintenance—many will grow thick enough to crowd out weeds. Extend the season by planting white-flowering daffodils or white grape hyacinths under the taller forms of artemisia.

RIGHT: ***Foliage with different textures, colors, and leaf shapes makes a garden interesting yet serene. Along a classic white picket fence, a planting of rosemary (*Rosmarinus officinalis*), mixed with silver-leaved perennials, grows tall and shrubby. This native of the Mediterranean loves the hot sun and well-drained soil of its home. In cooler climates, consider growing rosemary in a pot and overwintering it indoors.***

Chapter 4

Foliage in Autumn

I cannot imagine living in a part of the world where there is no autumn. The season of gourds and pumpkins, spiced cider and taffy apples, giant rolls of hay in farmer's fields and an uncanny harvest moon at night. Most of all, I'd miss nature's grand finale—the magical changing colors of the leaves. Of course I know all the scientific reasons that demystify the process, but don't bother me with details when I am driving, awestruck, through hills of amazing patchwork colors. Reason has nothing to do with my feelings about autumn.

Maples (**Acer **spp.) may well belong to the genus with the best autumn color, although the range and quality of color varies from species to species. Japanese maples (**Acer palmatum **forms and cultivars), such as the one shown here, have beautifully cut leaves and most have spectacular color, but they do require a more sheltered spot than the larger maples.

Take maple trees, for instance. I am not the biggest fan of maple trees as a general rule—they are fine in forests, but in a moderately sized suburban lot I think most of them are just too big. I have lived in three houses that were dwarfed by enormous Norway maples that completely blocked the sun, kept grass from growing, and kept us buried in leaves for months. Silver maples have pretty leaves but the trees are brittle and break easily; red maples have unpredictable color and sugar maples can be slow to establish. Most of the year that's my opinion of maples. But it is autumn as I write this and the red maples are setting my street on fire with their brilliant color, while sugar and Norway maples are adding depth and color to the woods near my house. Hmmm . . . come to think of it, I always did like paperbark maples, amur maples, trident maples—and maybe one of those new improved red maples would work in the front yard. Even the box elders are starting to look good.

Soon it will be winter, and like an addict craving a fix I get obsessive urges to plant trees and shrubs with autumn color. It's as if I need to store up the warmth of their brilliant colors to make it through the bleak months of black branches against snow-covered ground. Picturing the months of gray skies and beige lawns ahead, I want to savor every color of autumn. From neighbor's yards to neighboring hills, I don't have to look far to get a full palette of colorful effects. Star-shaped leaves of sweet gums blend gold, yellow, bronze, and red. Hotter than hot pink, the magenta leaves of burning bush are exclamation points against the burnished colors of 'Goldflame' spirea. Andorra junipers gradually change from green to bronze. Some hostas wilt while others turn a brilliant yellow; cranesbill geraniums color kaleidoscopically. The changing colors are everywhere—trees, vines, shrubs, perennials, grasses. It's as if they are having a final fling before shedding their skin.

People who never notice trees, who are immune to nature for most of the year, will stop dead in their tracks in front of the blazing colors of an autumn tree. Poets run for their pencils, musicians compose odes to the season, and artists try in vain to capture the essence of autumn. The garden is my canvas. All I do is give the plants a home, then sit back to enjoy the show. Won't you join me?

ABOVE: ***The vibrant red and orange autumn foliage of fothergilla (*Fothergilla major*) makes it a true garden favorite. This pretty shrub is also a star of spring, when its unusual, bristly, white flowers bloom.***

BELOW: *The maidenhair tree or ginkgo (*Ginkgo biloba*) has beautiful fan-shaped leaves that become brilliant yellow in autumn. Before purchasing a ginkgo, make sure the nursery can guarantee that it is a male plant. The fruit of female ginkgo trees is notoriously odiferous, that is, it stinks. The ginkgo has two more edifying claims to fame: first, even though it is deciduous it is classified as a conifer. Second, ginkgo trees would have been familiar to the dinosaurs of* Jurassic Park *because they have existed, unchanged, since long before that time.*

Why Do Leaves Change Color?

We take the changes of the year for granted until we go someplace that doesn't share our seasonal conditions. In the same way, we take it for granted when leaves change color, die, and fall from the tree. Gardeners usually take note if it is a good year or a bad year for autumn color, but many do not really understand how or why the color changes take place.

Several chemicals determine the colors of leaves throughout the seasons. The best known of these is chlorophyll, which goes through a continual process of manufacture and destruction throughout the cycle of a leaf. Think of chlorophyll as the green crayon that colors leaves, while carotins and xanthophyll are the yellow crayons and anthocyanins are the red crayons. In some red- and yellow-leaved plants, leaf coloration is very bright in spring but becomes duller as the season progresses. This is due to the production of chlorophyll—as the production of chlorophyll decreases, the bright coloration becomes visible again. In addition to chemical changes in the leaf, coloration can be affected by soil pH, fertilization, climate, and moisture levels in the soil.

Red coloring is related to the presence of sugars and tannins in the leaf, so the coloration tends to be better in years when autumn days are warm and sunny, which encourages production of sugars and tannins, and evenings are cool, which allows them to accumulate in the plant. Yellow coloring is much more prevalent, and its presence is primarily related to the absence of chlorophyll. Often a combination of factors will determine the coloring of a particular species from one year to the next, despite the basic chemical content of the leaf. A few species are particularly variable, but poor autumn coloration is usually related to wet weather without the necessary sunlight to ensure sugar production. Brown coloration is not connected with chemicals in the leaf—it simply means the leaf is dead or dying.

LEFT: ***Just as the sky explodes with color before sunset, forests and gardens light up with blazing autumn color immediately before winter sets in.***

Trees, Shrubs, and Perennials with Fantastic Autumn Color

For many gardeners, the incredible color changes of autumn render it the most anticipated season of the year. As the weather cools and winter approaches inexorably, we seem to have more time to appreciate the gradual color changes—at least in years when the leaves don't fall off the trees all at once.

I have actually met people who went out of their way to avoid plant-ing anything that would exhibit autumn color. They found the brilliant shades too jarring, which is incomprehensible to me, but then I am fond of purple and magenta, too. I can't imagine a foliage gardener who doesn't crave autumn color, but if you are one of that mysterious breed, avoid the plants on the following pages at all costs. It will leave more for the rest of us.

TOP: ***The richly colored leaves of this Japanese maple (*****Acer palmatum 'Atropurpureum'*****) are dazzling rather than gaudy. If you can offer these compact trees a sheltered spot they are sure to become garden treasures.***

BOTTOM: ***Foliage of the Chinese pistachio (*****Pistacia chinesis*****) gradually evolves from scarlet to purple in the autumn. Unfortunately, this highly ornamental tree is only hardy in Zones 7 to 9.***

TREES

Acer × *freemani* 'Autumn Blaze' (hybrid red maple)

Acer capillipes (snakebark maple)

Acer ginnala and cultivars 'Embers', 'Flame' (amur maple)

Acer japonicum and cultivars (full moon maple)

Acer palmatum and cultivars (Japanese maple)

Fraxinus americana including cultivars 'Cimmaron', 'Autumn Blaze', 'Autumn Purple' (white ash)

Fraxinus pensylvanica 'Dakota Centennial' (green ash)

Ginkgo biloba 'Shangri-la' (ginkgo)

Liquidambar styraciflua (sweet gum)

Nyssa sylvatica (black gum, tupelo)

Oxydendron arboreum (sourwood)

Parrotia persica (parrotia)

Acer platanoides 'Crimson King', 'Norwegian Sunset' (Norway maple)

Acer rubrum 'October Glory' ('October Glory' red maple)

Acer saccharum including cultivars 'Seneca Chief', 'Green Mountain', 'Bonfire' (sugar maple)

Amelanchier × *grandiflora* 'Autumn Brilliance' (apple serviceberry)

Amelanchier laevis (serviceberry)

Cercidiphyllum japonicum (katsuratree)

Cornus florida (flowering dogwood)

Cornus mas 'Golden Glory' (corneliancherry dogwood)

Pistachia chinensis (Chinese pistache)

Pyrus calleryana 'Chanticleer', 'Autumn Blaze', etc. (flowering callery pear)

Quercus coccinea (scarlet oak)

Quercus palustris (swamp white oak)

Quercus rubra (red oak)

Sassafras albidum (sassafrass)

ABOVE: ***Persian parottia (*****Parottia persica*****) has graceful arching branches covered with foliage that turn yellow, orange, and red in autumn.*** LEFT: ***There are scores of Japanese maples (*****Acer palmatum*****) with brilliant autumn color, excellent form, and intricate foliage. Virtually all Japanese maples add interest and distinction to the landscape.***

ABOVE: ***Redvein enkianthus (*****Enkianthus campanulatus*****) leaves blaze orange and scarlet in autumn.***
OPPOSITE: ***With more than two hundred ornamental viburnums in cultivation, it is amazing how few gardeners are aware of the diverse and decorative plants this genus has to offer. The leaves of European cranberrybush viburnum (*****Viburnum opulus*****) are similar to maple leaves in shape and, as shown here, they have equally brilliant autumn color.***

SHRUBS

Aronia arbutifolia 'Brilliantissima' (red chokeberry)

Berberis thunbergii and cultivars (barberry)

Cotinus coggygria 'Flame' (purple smoketree)

Cornus sericea (red-osier dogwood)

Cotoneaster salicifolius 'Autumn Fire' (willowleaf cotoneaster)

Enkianthus campanulatus (redvein enkianthus)

Euonymus alata 'Compacta' (dwarf burning bush)

Fothergilla major (syn. *F. monticola*) (fothergilla)

Nandina domestica (heavenly bamboo)

Itea virginica (Virginia sweetspire)

Spirea × bumalda 'Gold Flame'

Viburnum carlesii (Koreanspice viburnum)

Viburnum opulus (European cranberrybush viburnum)

PERENNIALS, VINES, AND GRASSES

Amsonia hubrectii (Arkansas amsonia)

Bergenia 'Bressingham Ruby' (heartleaf bergenia)

Euphorbia griffithii 'Fireglow' (Griffith's spurge)

Gaultheria procumbens (creeping wintergreen)

Geranium sanguineum (bloody cranesbill)

Hosta (selected cultivars) (hosta)

Miscanthus sinensis var. *purpurascens* (Japanese silver grass)

Parthenocissus tricuspidata (Boston ivy)

AUTUMN COLOR GARDEN

Planning an autumn color garden with an emphasis on foliage could be compared to putting a kid with a handful of change in an old-fashioned penny candy store. There is almost too much to choose from! This garden was planned for a house on a suburban lot with no planting in the back. Gardeners who already have a few trees or large shrubs with good autumn color can adapt part of the plan while leaving out the expensive part—the trees. A word of caution: many trees that exhibit beautiful autumn color will become very large shade trees, so be sure to allow them lots of room to grow.

To prevent lawnmower damage and competition from grass roots, dig out the grass in a circle about 6 feet (1.8m) in diameter around each tree. These tree rings can be covered in mulch (about 3 inches [7cm] deep) or planted with annuals or groundcovers. The maples will eventually shade out most groundcovers, but I have suggested underplanting the ginkgo (which may take a few years to really look great) with a lacy-leaved hybrid foamflower that will gradually spread.

The ginkgo, which has been around since prehistoric times, is unique in many ways. The fan-shaped leaves, which turn golden in autumn, are so ornamental that they are often used in jewelry and fabric designs. Many gardeners are surprised to learn that the ginkgo is actually a conifer. The cultivar in this plan, 'Princeton Sentry'™, is very narrow growing, ultimately reaching about 60 feet (18m) high and 20 feet (6m) wide. It is important to note that this is a male cultivar, since female plants (often unlabeled in nurseries and catalogs), will eventually bear foul-smelling fruits.

The maples in this plan were chosen with care because there is huge difference between trees in this genus. The 'Autumn Blaze' maple is a relatively new hybrid that took the good but unpredictable color of red maples, combined it with the fast-growing but weak-branched silver maples, and came up with a tree that exhibits the best traits of both species, apparently without the weaknesses. 'Autumn Blaze' is drought tolerant and will eventually reach a height of 50 feet (15m) with a spread of about 45 feet (13.5m). The brilliant orange-red autumn color may not be apparent until the tree is a few years old. The amur maple is often trimmed for use as a hedge, but to me it is better suited as a small ornamental tree with its attractive foliage, brilliant autumn color, hardiness, and an ultimate size of only 20 to 25 feet (6 to 7.5m).

The golden larch is one of the very few deciduous conifers—in other words, its needles fall in winter—but it is really one of horticulture's hidden treasures. While it may not take the heat or cold of North America's extremeties, the middle regions (Zones 4 or 5 to 7) should readily support the needs of this species. The golden larch is a slow grower that may eventually reach 60 feet (18m) tall if grown in well-drained but moist soil on the acidic side. A native of China, the open form of this tree makes a distinctive statement in the landscape; although it is rare, it is becoming more readily available in the landscape trade.

Compact burning bush is both fairly common and easily obtained, for all the best reasons. It is easy to propagate and grow, and will survive in a variety of soils and climatic situations. This shrub is often used as a tightly pruned hedge but I prefer its natural form; the compact burning bush will keep to a manageable size that should not require much pruning. It is easy to be overwhelmed by the outstanding autumn color, which can be more magenta than red at times, but the corky bark and orangey red seeds can also be eyecatching. (Note: the cultivar 'Compactus' may exhibit variable traits such as bark that is considerably less "corky" than the species.)

A few of the perennials featured were selected for their foliage and structure more than their autumn color. Yucca, for example, has a long flowering period but its main attraction is the sharp, spiky foliage that makes it stand out in the landscape.

Yucca will grow in even poor soil, but think twice before putting it in a mixed border. In good soil, it has a tendency to spread and the roots are all but impossible to completely remove. (When I was relandscaping my present house, a neighbor offered me three yuccas he had thinned out. I had just removed some foundation plantings and knew it would be awhile before I could afford to install phase two, so I welcomed the plants. I am now battling to remove a constantly renewed crop of baby yuccas from the base of my new Koreanspice viburnums, two years after removing the parent plants.)

'Autumn Joy' sedum (although no longer technically a sedum) is one of the best known perennials, in part because it is easy to grow and in part because of its ornamental value throughout the seasons. The flowers start out green, gradually progressing through shades of pink and rose to burgundy or bronze, and the foliage always looks great. 'Perfect Peach Glory' is a new daylily cultivar that I think offsets the deep purple foliage of snakeroot nicely. It is a repeat bloomer, but the foliage of daylilies adds a distinctive touch even when they are not in bloom.

Arkansas amsonia may be hard to find but it will be well worth the search. The tickseed, sage, plumbago, and ornamental grasses featured may be available through local nurseries, but if not, are readily available by mail order.

I have included containers of ornamental kale and globe artichoke on the deck in this plan, but they could easily be included in a perennial border. The globe artichoke is best purchased as a plant rather than started from seed, unless you are extremely patient. Although it is related to the prolific thistle, globe artichoke is a perennial vegetable that may take a few years to mature. Ornamental kale is usually sold as an annual, but with a little mulching it may survive for several years. Ornamental cabbage and kale are available in a variety of colors; they are often used at the front of a perennial border or in combination with chrysanthemums.

ABOVE: ***In the Midwest, winged euonymus (*****Euonymus alatus*****), burning bush, spindle tree, or whatever you choose to call it is the shrub for autumn color. Although the precise color may vary slightly from plant to plant and from species to cultivar, the result is always the same—spectacular! The color is alternately described as "brilliant red," "fluorescent pinkish red," or "bright deep red," but to me it could almost be called magenta.***

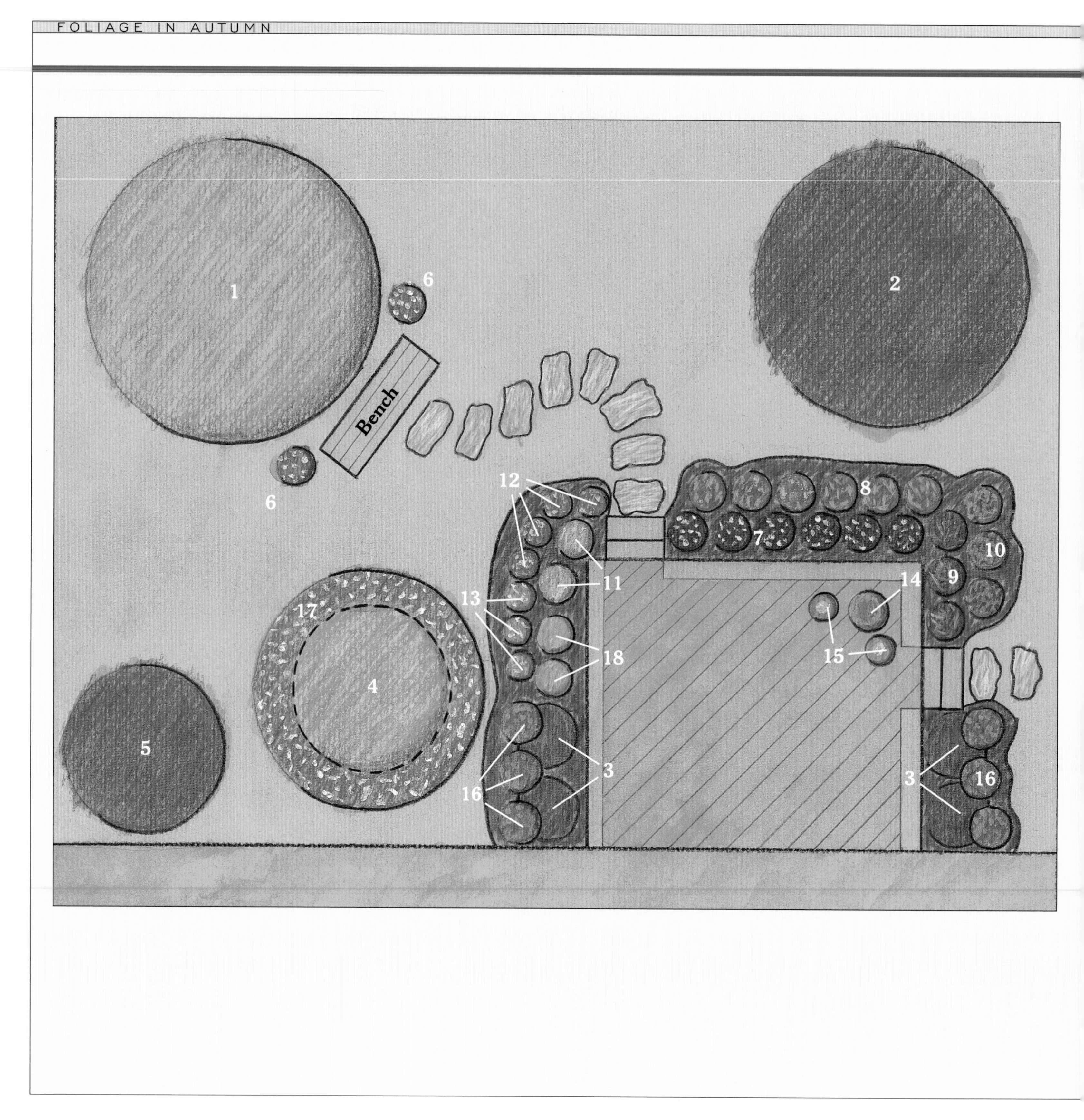
1
2
3
4
5
6
7
8
9
10
11
12
13
14
15
16
17
18
Bench

PLANT LIST

SUGGESTED QUANTITIES ARE NOTED AFTER EACH PLANT NAME.

1. *Pseudolarix amabilis* (golden larch)—1
2. *Acer × freemanii* ('Autumn Blaze' maple)—1
3. *Euonymus alatus* 'Compactus' (dwarf burning bush)—4
4. *Ginkgo biloba* 'Princeton Sentry' ('Princeton Sentry' ginkgo)—1
5. *Acer ginnala* (amur maple)—1
6. *Yucca filamentosa* (Adam's needle)—2
7. *Cimicifuga racemosa* 'Hillside Black Beauty' (snakeroot)—6
8. *Hemerocallis* × 'Perfect Peach Glory' (hybrid daylily 'Perfect Peach Glory')—7
9. *Miscanthus sinensis* 'Purpurescens' (flame grass)—3
10. *Hylotelephium* × 'Autumn Joy' (syn. *Sedum* × 'Autumn Joy') ('Autumn Joy' sedum or stonecrop)—3
11. *Salvia officinalis* 'Aurea' (golden sage)—2
12. *Coreopsis verticillata* 'Zagreb' (threadleaf tickseed)—4
13. *Festuca cinerea* 'Meerblau' (blue fescue)—3
14. *Cynara scolymus* (globe artichoke)—1
15. *Brassica aleracea* (ornamental kale)—2
16. *Ceratostigma plumbaginoides* (plumbago)—12
17. *Tiarella* × 'Filigree Lace' (hybrid foamflower)—6
18. *Amsonia hubrectii* (Arkansas amsonia)—2

ABOVE: ***'Autumn Joy' stonecrop (*****Hylotelephium** × ***'Autumn Joy') has lush, succulent foliage for most of the season, but bears red flower heads in late summer that deepen to cinnamon as they dry. A good companion for ornamental grasses, 'Autumn Joy' stonecrop offers many months of interest in the garden.***

Japanese Maples

Some of the most beautiful leaves in the plant world can be found on Japanese maples. That may be my own opinion, but I don't think many gardeners would argue the point. Beautifully cut leaves, outstanding autumn color, dramatic form—what more can you ask of a tree? Well, it would be nice if they were a little more hardy, since most will only survive a winter up to Zones 5 or 6. And they need a little protection from sun and wind, but who's complaining? Especially since Japanese maples have the added benefit of compact size—even the largest would fit with ease in city or suburban gardens, while the smallest are suitable for containers, rock gardens, and even bonsai.

ABOVE: ***The leaves of Japanese maples (*****Acer palmatum*****) vary tremendously from one cultivar to the next. The thinly elegant leaf pictured here belongs to the dwarf cultivar 'Villa Taranto'. While it may be difficult to locate a particular cultivar for your garden, it would be hard to think of a Japanese maple that is not elegant and ornamental.***
OPPOSITE: ***The two Japanese maples at right,*** **Acer palmatum** ***'Dissectum' and 'Suminagashi', exemplify the differences that can be found in size, habit, form, and foliage of cultivars in this exotic species.***

The coral bark maple (*Acer palmatum* 'Sango Kaku', syn. 'Senkaki') has branches that rival the best redtwig dogwoods in winter. The golden full moon maple (*Acer shirasawanum* 'Aureum') has breathtaking foliage, with an ultimate height and spread of about 15 feet (4.5m). Many Japanese maples are recommended for autumn color, including *Acer japonicum* 'Viti-folium' and *Acer palmatum* 'Red Filigree Lace'. Several cultivars of laceleaf Japanese maples (*Acer palmatum* var. *dissectum*) are stunning: 'Seiryu', 'Toyo Nishiki', and 'Tamukeyama'.

There is even a fernleaf Japanese maple (*Acer japonicum* forma *aconitifolium*), while the lion's mane maple (*Acer palmatum* 'Shigashura') goes to the other extreme, bearing very thick, wrinkled foliage. Several Japanese maples have unusual variegated foliage, such as *Acer palmatum* 'Orido Nishiki', 'Ukigumo', and 'Beni Schichihenge'. Better-known Japanese maples include *Acer palmatum* 'Bloodgood', 'Oshio Beni', 'Ozakazuki', 'Dissectum Atropurpureum', and 'Waterfall'.

Japanese maples are so ornamental, they should be included in any garden focusing on foliage if a suitably sheltered location can be found.

RIGHT: ***Some of the most ornamental landscape plants are not available at every garden center, but they are definitely worth seeking out. The sourwood tree (*Oxydendron arboreum*) with fragrant flowers and excellent autumn color, is one example shown here; another is the dwarf fothergilla (*Fothergilla gardenii*), which performs equally well in sun or shade.***

Chapter 5

A Winter Wonderland

Winter is not my favorite season. Skiers can have it, especially once the holidays have passed and the winter blahs set in. I lived in England for several years, and while I rarely saw the legendary "pea-soup" fog I'd heard so much about, I did experience a damp cold that cut right through to the bone. Coming from Chicago, though, I found one big plus in spending wintertime in England—the crocuses came up before Valentine's Day! The delicate pale green shoots struggling up through the soil helped make the time move more quickly into the eagerly awaited spring.

The essence of the winter garden is captured in this snow-covered tableau. Spidery flowers of hybrid witchhazel (*Hamamelis × intermedia*) mingle in frozen splendor with the bright red fruits of winterberry (*Ilex verticillata*) and branches stark against the snow.

Cincinnati, my current home, has winters that are usually a bit milder and shorter than those Chicago endures, but not as mild as England's winters usually are. Bloom times are considerably earlier than in Chicago, but there are still all those months of winter. As a person who only puts up with winter because of the wonders of spring and autumn, I have had to cultivate an appreciation of winter gardens. Browsing through a book about the joys of gardens in winter, I ruefully noted that most of the gardens pictured were photographed in England or California. What are the alternatives for a gardener who would love to see the hellebores and snowdrops so lovingly portrayed in books? Even the hardiest plants have trouble pushing their way up through a mound of snow.

I will be the first to admit there is beauty to be found in snow and ice. Watching the woods turned into a fairyland by an overnight ice storm, it's easy to believe in winter's magic. (Just don't think of the damage the ice is doing to those poor trees.) The spun-sugar look of freshly fallen snow is also easier to enjoy when you aren't outside in the cold shovelling driveways, digging out bent-over conifers, and watching passing cars turn the pristine white to dirty gray. I have had to train my eyes to find beauty in the winter landscape.

I have learned that in the winter landscape form and structure are of primary importance. Trees that are dressed in a dense cloak of leaves throughout most of the year are revealed to have a strong skeleton of interesting branches. Without the distraction of leaves, bark takes on a new importance. Conifers discard their summer camouflage and move into prominence. Tall grasses seem to freeze as they sway, while some structurally sound perennials stand firm against winter winds. Seedheads, rose hips, and berries of all kinds take on dramatic significance. Neatly trimmed hedges of yew no longer seem to simply frame the garden, they define it.

In winter, every stone and brick takes on special power. The brick adds warmth while stones and concrete pavers blend with the neutral colors of the season. Even gravel paths look artistic against the snow. Every garden structure is highlighted in winter—whether it is a gazebo, bridge, deck, arbor, trellis, wall, pond, or a simple bench. A large stone urn, a sundial, a birdbath, a trough container garden, a brick wall covered in Virginia creeper—all of these take on a certain elegance against a backdrop of snow. Statuary and garden ornaments—those that are able to withstand freeze and thaw conditions—become focal points, without foliage and flowers to distract the eye.

A limited number of perennials look good through the winter, but an incredible number of trees and shrubs look just great without their leaves on. Conifers—including much more than the ubiquitous "Christmas tree"—can be wonderful in a winter garden if selected with care. A huge, fast-growing conifer placed precisely where it will block the winter sun from the house will defeat the purpose. Look beyond the Christmas tree shape to discover the wonders of dwarf conifers and others that grow in a gnarly fashion. Trees and perennials that have wonderful flowers in spring may not present the most attractive silhouette in winter. Try to plant at least one tree or shrub that will shine in each season.

When food is scarce in winter, assorted wildlife may decide to check out your garden. It is very cheering to see colorful birds and little creatures enjoying home-grown winter snacks such as the fruits of some crabapples, but the beautiful white-tailed deer can quickly wear out its welcome. Through trial and error and by comparing notes with other local gardeners, you can usually build up a picture of plants the deer are partial to, and plants they will leave alone.

Foliage may be limited in winter, but with the added details of fruit, bark, form, and structure, a garden in winter can become a thing of beauty.

OPPOSITE: ***The sprawling multiple branches of a mature katsura tree (*****Cercidiphyllum japonicum*****) make a bold statement in this winter landscape. An excellent and underused tree, katsura tree needs some space to develop to its true potential. It has something to offer for every season, and in winter the shaggy bark of older trees gives them added character. The weeping form, 'Pendula', is much smaller and perfectly suited for a residential landscape, but it can be very hard to find.***

A TEXTURED TAPESTRY FOR WINTER

The foliage in a winter garden takes on an aspect of otherworldliness when it is encased in ice, glazed with frost, or outlined in snow. Deciduous trees caught by an early freeze look overburdened with the weight of frozen brown leaves, and evergreens hold pride of place. Groundcover evergreens may vanish under a mantle of snow in some regions, but there is more to winter than "Christmas trees." Broadleaf evergreens may be more common in warmer parts of the country, but an increasing number are being bred for less hospitable climates. The winter-flowering perennials so beloved by English gardeners would shrivel in the presence of a North American winter—even in many of the milder regions—so pass over those tender plants and select perennials whose form, even when frozen, will be a highlight in the winter garden. Some ornamental grasses—not all—look almost as good coated in ice as they do in their midsummer prime.

The river birch cultivar 'Heritage' is recommended both for its ornamental peeling bark and for its resistance to birch borer and other pests that plague white birches. Select a clump with at least three to five trunks for the best effect, or plant smaller clumps close together. There are numerous redtwig dogwood cultivars available, but many have only mediocre winter coloring. The Westonbirt dogwood has twigs that positively glow in winter, while the bloodtwig dogwood has twigs that start out yellow at the base and turn red at the tips. All redtwig dogwoods benefit from the occasional thinning of branches; the brilliant color will gradually fade unless you cut back the branches periodically.

The cutleaf sumac features elegantly defined leaves, interesting branching, excellent autumn color, and fruits that are attractive to birds. It is not picky as to soil or growing conditions; it will gradually form a large clump about 10 feet (3m) high. Harry Lauder's walking stick is a freak show of a plant that has the appeal of a sad-eyed clown even when its trademark branches are hidden by foliage. It can become messy if suckers are not routinely pruned, but in winter it will steal the show. The ornamental grasses featured in this plan are a plus to the garden in every season, although in winter they are real standouts. Snow may hide the attraction of creeping cotoneaster and groundcover junipers, but on snowless days they will add an extra dimension to the garden.

Brewer's weeping spruce is an old variety that is still available, despite countless newer introductions, because of its elegant form and weeping habit. Sturdy, solemn, and long-lived, it will become the keystone of this winter garden. The glossy leaves and bright berries of the two meserve hollies, 'China Girl' and its pollinator 'China Boy', will add bright spots of color.

Form and structure are always essential (picture a human walking around without a skeleton to give it form!), but in the winter garden they become sublime. Without the ever-present green, without the distraction of bright colors and showy flowers, details such as bark and branching, seedheads and berries take on a new importance. Hedges that are virtually invisible in summer become a clear framework in winter; fences and walls that are hidden by greenery in warmer months are brought into high relief under the pale winter sun. Brick takes on a new warmth, concrete wears an icy sheen, and wooden structures seem rugged and rough against the snow. Winter shows a garden first thing in the morning—in its underwear, with hair uncombed and pouches evident under the eyes. Like an old woman whose beauty is defined by strong bone structure, the magnificence of a winter garden is revealed unadorned.

OPPOSITE: ***The showy plumes of dormant Japanese silver grass (*Miscanthus sinensis*) make beautiful accents in the winter landscape. There are many versatile cultivars and varieties of Japanese silver grass that add excitement to the landscape all year round.***

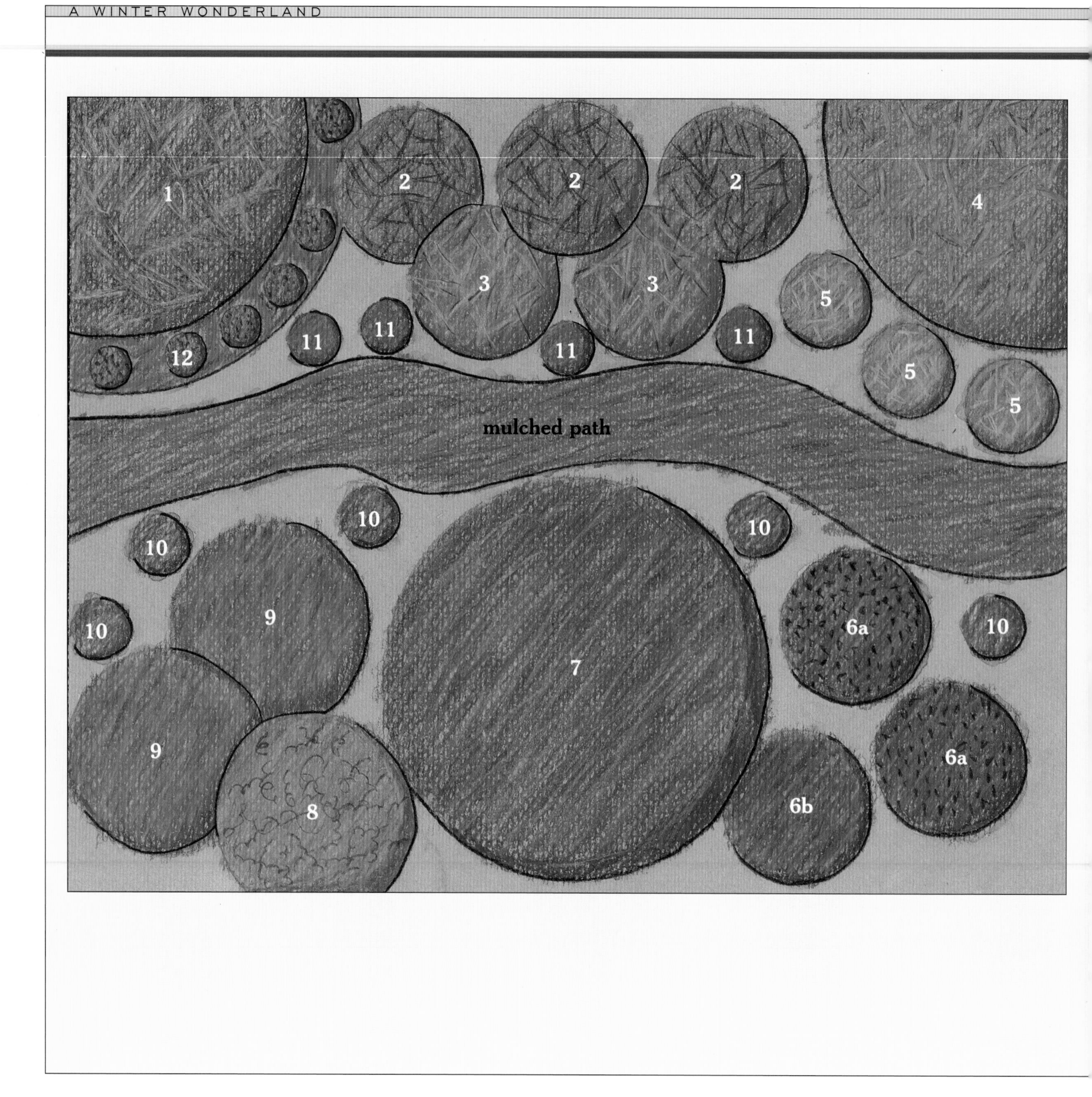
1
2
2
2
4
3
3
5
11
11
11
11
12
5
5
mulched path
10
10
10
10
10
9
7
6a
9
8
6b
6a

PLANT LIST

SUGGESTED QUANTITIES ARE NOTED AFTER EACH PLANT NAME.

1. *Betula nigra* 'Heritage' ('Heritage' river birch)—1

2. *Cornus alba* 'Sibirica' (Westonbirt dogwood)—3

3. *Cornus sanguinea* 'Winter Beauty' (bloodtwig dogwood)—2

4. *Rhus typhina* 'Laciniata' (cutleaf sumac)—1

5. *Miscanthus sinensis* 'Gracillimus' (maiden grass)—3

6a. *Ilex* × 'China Girl' (meserve hybrid holly)—2

6b. *Ilex* × 'China Boy' (meserve hybrid holly)—1

7. *Picea breweriana* (brewer's weeping spruce)—1

8. *Corylus avellana* 'Contorta' (Harry Lauder's walking stick)—1

9. *Molina caerulea* var. *arundinacea* 'Skyracer' (tall moorgrass)—2

10. *Juniperus horizontalis* 'Wiltonii' (blue rug juniper)—5

11. *Juniperus horizontalis* 'Blue Chip' (blue chip juniper)—4

12. *Cotoneaster adpressus* var. *praecox* (creeping cotoneaster)—5

ABOVE: ***Glowing blood red in the setting sun, Westonbirt dogwood (*****Cornus alba*** ***'Sibirica') provides unexpectedly brilliant color in the winter landscape.***

Plants with Decorative Bark

There are many trees and shrubs with attractive stems or bark, but it is easy to overlook them when the garden is full of foliage and flowers. A little judicial pruning can help make the most of these plants.

Red- and yellowtwig dogwoods are fast-growing shrubs that send up lots of new stems every year, eventually forming a dense thicket. By pruning out some of the older branches every year, you can keep these shrubs from becoming ungainly; cutting the branches of red- and yellowtwig dogwoods back to 2 or 3 feet (60 to 90cm) helps keep the color bright. In the case of trees with decorative bark, such as lacebark pine, it makes sense to prune away the lower branches so the attractive bark becomes more visible.

The trees and shrubs listed here all have something to offer to the winter garden, whether it is colorful branches, exfoliating bark, unusual shapes and textures, a glossy sheen, or a graceful branching pattern. In addition to the plants listed, most weeping trees are very effective in a winter landscape. Please note that some beautiful trees, like eucalyptus and strawberry tree, have very attractive bark but would not be hardy in cold-winter areas.

LEFT: ***In the winter, when trees do not have the distraction of leaves, peeling bark takes on a distinctive beauty of its own.***
OPPOSITE: ***Structural elements such as this rustic bridge become focal points in the winter landscape. In the foreground, a stand of 'Heritage' river birch (*Betula nigra *'Heritage') displays the attractive exfoliating bark that makes this species so popular. While all river birches have interesting bark, the cultivar 'Heritage' has unique, pale cream- to salmon-colored bark. Far more resistant to pests and diseases than other birches, river birches in general perform best in uniformly moist, acidic soil.***

Acer capillipes (snakebark maple)
Acer griseum (paperbark maple)
Acer palmatum (Japanese maple, particularly *Acer palmatum* 'Sango Kaku', syn. 'Senkaki', the coral bark maple)
Acer pensylvanicum 'Erythrocladum' (striped maple)
Acer tegmentosum (Manchustriped maple)
Betula nigra 'Heritage' ('Heritage' river birch)
Betula platyphylla var. *japonica* 'Whitespire' (Japanese white birch)
Cornus alba 'Sibirica' (Westonbirt dogwood)
Cornus controversa 'Variegata' (giant variegated dogwood)
Cornus sanguinea (bloodtwig dogwood)
Cornus stolonifera 'Flaviramea' (yellowtwig red osier dogwood)
Cornus stolonifera 'Isanti' (red osier dogwood)
Corylus avellana 'Contorta' (Harry Lauder's walking stick)
Euonymus alatus (burning bush, spindle tree)
Kerria japonica (Japanese kerria)
Pinus bungeana (lacebark pine)
Pinus densiflora 'Umbraculifera' (syn. 'Tanyosho', umbrella pine)
Platanus acerifolia (London planetree)
Prunus maacki (Manchurian cherry)
Prunus serrula (peeling bark cherry)
Rhus typhina (staghorn sumac)
Rubus cockburnianus (white-stemmed brambles)
Salix alba 'Britzensis' (scarlet willow)
Salix alba 'Vitellina' (golden willow)
Salix irrorata (white-stemmed willow)
Salix matsudana 'Tortuosa' (corkscrew willow)

Winter's Flora: Fruits, Seedheads, and Dried Flowers

Unless you live in a very temperate zone, winter and flowers don't go together. As I browse through books on winter gardening and four-season gardening, all too often I find that the plants they recommend are not hardy beyond Zone 7. If you live in an area where winter means cold, you learn to find beauty in other winter "flora." The bright colors of fruiting shrubs and trees, interesting seedheads and catkins, colorful hips of old roses, and the stiff flower heads of some perennials all combine to make a winter garden rich with color and form. Some shrubs, like witchhazels and the corneliancherry dogwood, flower when it still feels like winter. The plants listed here can usually be relied on to make the most of a winter garden.

ABOVE: ***Some gardeners call the colorful heads of ornamental cabbage (*****Brassica** ***spp.) flowers, others call it foliage. Whatever you call it, ornamental cabbage has soared in popularity in recent years and is now often seen as a companion plant to autumn-flowering chrysanthemums. Unlike the mums, though, ornamental cabbage looks great all summer, too.*** RIGHT: ***The bright orange-red berries of scarlet firethorn (*****Pyracantha coccinea*****) bring spots of color to the garden even when dusted with snow. The berries are a favorite of birds, who may also relish the thorny branches for nesting.*** OPPOSITE: ***In order for a crabapple to have ornamental winter fruit, the fruit must remain on the tree long enough to be ornamental—this is called "persistent" fruiting. The 'Winter Gold' crabapple (*****Malus** × ***'Winter Gold') shown is considered one of the best "yellow-fruited" crabapples. The lemony yellow fruit retains its color even after a hard frost and it is not unusual to find fruit still on the tree in February.***

Abeliophyllum distichum (white forsythia)

Alchemilla mollis (lady's mantle)

Alnus cordata (Italian alder)

Alnus incana 'Aurea' (golden gray alder)

Berberis thunbergii 'Sparkle' (Japanese barberry)

Bergenia cordifolia hybrids and cultivars such as 'Bressingham Ruby', 'Evening Glow', 'Sunningdale' (heartleaf bergenia)

Brassica oleracea (ornamental kale)

Callicarpa dichotoma (purple beautyberry)

Cornus mas 'Golden Glory' (corneliancherry dogwood)

Cotoneaster adpressus (creeping cotoneaster; also *C.a.* var. *praecox*)

Hamamelis × *intermedia* cultivars, i.e. 'Arnold Promise', 'Diane', 'Fire Charm', 'Jelena', 'Ruby Glow' (hybrid witchhazel)

Hamamelis mollis (Chinese witchhazel)

Hamamelis virginiana (common witchhazel)

Hamamelis vernalis (vernal witchhazel)

Hylotelephium × 'Autumn Joy' (formerly *Sedum* × 'Autumn Joy'; Stonecrop)

Ilex × 'Sparkleberry'(hybrid winterberry; use *Ilex* × 'Apollo' to pollinate)

Ilex verticillata 'Winter Red' (winterberry; needs pollinator)

Mahonia aquifolium (Oregon grapeholly; recommended cultivars include 'Compactum', 'Golden Abundance', 'Emerald', 'King's Ransom')

Malus species and hybrids including 'Bob White', 'Donald Wyman', 'Katherine', 'Makamik', 'Ormiston Roy', 'Red Jade', 'Sissipuk', 'Winter Gold', *Malus zumi* 'Calocarpa' (crabapple)

Miscanthus sinensis 'Morning Light' (Japanese silver grass)

Prunus subhirtella 'Autumnalis' (autumn cherry)

Pyracantha coccinea (scarlet firethorn, including hybrids and cultivars such as 'Apache', 'Baker's Red', 'Chadwickii', 'Lalandei', 'Rutgers', 'Teton')

Rhus chinensis 'September Beauty' (Chinese sumac)

Rosa 'Frau Dagmar Hastrup', 'Hansa', 'Scabrosa' (rugosa rose cultivars)

Rosa rubrifolia (redleaf rose)

Salix gracilistyla var. *melanostachys* (black pussy willow)

Symphoricarpos albus (common snowberry)

Symphoricarpos × *chenaultii* 'Hancock' (hybrid Chenault coralberry)

Chapter 6

Conifers as Ornamentals

Rich and Susan Eyre, co-owners of Rich's Foxwillow Pines Nursery in Woodstock, Illinois, once stood before the central region of the American Conifer Society and confessed their addiction to conifers. They went through a whole twelve-step program explaining how they had progressed from interest to obsession. The rueful laughter of the crowd made it clear that they were preaching to the converted—all present had discovered the fascination of conifers.

Mugo pines can be found in just about any garden center in the country, but you'll need to track down specialty nurseries to find this wonderful cultivar called 'Carsten'* (Pinus mugo *'Carsten', sometimes 'Carsten's Gold'). A nicely contained dwarf form, the foliage of the 'Carsten' mugo pine turns a golden color in winter. In the picture here, the needles look as if they have been dipped in brilliant gold paint.

Even non-gardeners will admit to a certain awe when driving through forests of spruce, fir, or pine. The majesty of redwoods, probably the world's tallest trees, is undeniable. Few people are lucky enough to live in the mountains and look out to see these wonders every day. Most of us live in condos, townhouses, duplexes, brownstones, one-up/one-down Georgians, or suburban ranches or colonials on lots that measure in fractions of an acre instead of multiples. Instead of mountain or ocean views, we overlook asphalt streets, tall buildings, or other houses on lots just like ours.

It's easy to be tempted to plant conifers that look wonderful in the nursery at 6 feet (1.8m) tall and 4 feet (1.2m) wide. In a world where people move a lot, you may not be living there when the same tree is 70 feet (21m) tall and 40 feet (12m) wide. Think about it—very few homeowners really consider the ultimate size of a tree when they plant it. Those who do are most likely to focus on the ultimate height of the tree, forgetting that as the tree grows taller, it will also grow proportionately wider. It is partly for this reason that so many gardeners seek out dwarf conifers—not full-size conifers that grow very slowly, but true dwarfs, bred or selected to stay small.

Even reputable nurseries have been known to label conifers as dwarf when they are anything but. It is not always easy to verify the nursery's information, either, since many plant reference books have a scarcity of information on conifers. *Krussman's Manual of Cultivated Conifers* is very helpful, but it is unlikely that you'll find it on the shelves of your local library. If you have a public garden, an arboretum, or a garden club library nearby, it will be a better resource than a public library. Really good bookstores do stock useful reference books, but unfortunately the best reference books can cost as much as a tree. Another possibility is to contact the local

chapter of the American Conifer Society. Their members range from average homeowners with an interest in conifers to nurseries who specialize in growing rare conifers to researchers and hybridizers who are working to introduce new cultivars. The society can refer you to experts who live in your area or give you advice on the tree you are considering.

This may be more work than you are prepared to put into selecting a tree or shrub. Fair enough. But remember that a few carefully selected trees can add tremendously to the value of a house, as well as adding to your enjoyment. A tree that is too big, prone to disease, or easily affected by cold, drought, or other extremes is going to be a giant-size headache in years to come. It's like the old saying—dig a $10 hole for a $1 tree (obviously, it is a very old saying). It means that preparing a good hole to start with will ensure that your dollar is well spent. A little research before you buy can be equally valuable.

The conifers recommended throughout this book are among the "best" conifers available (if you can have a "best" in nature, that is). I wish I could guarantee that every conifer I mention will do well in every region, but that is not possible. I have tried to avoid mentioning conifers that have a bad reputation or a propensity to pests or diseases. I have also made a point of listing newer, exciting, and attractive conifers even if they may be more difficult to find. The more people start asking for better trees, the more nurseries will strive to provide them.

Conifers are a valuable addition to any landscape, for every season. You may start with one but—you have been warned—once you discover the world of conifers, you won't look back.

OPPOSITE: ***The palette of color displayed in this conifer garden should dispel, once and for all, the notion that "evergreens" are dull, Christmas-tree-shaped, and green. Although a garden of conifers is interesting during all seasons, it really comes into its own in the winter.*** RIGHT: ***Garden designers are fond of combining blue conifers with burgundy, bronze, purple, or wine-colored deciduous trees and shrubs. Here, "groundcover" juniper,* Juniperus squamata *'Blue Carpet', spills gracefully across the foreground as the jewel tones of a Japanese maple (*Acer palmatum *'Dissectum Garnet') provide contrasting texture and added depth.***

ABOVE: *There are many cultivars of blue spruce (*Picea pungens *forma* glauca*) available, from traditional "Christmas tree" shapes to narrow, columnar forms to dwarf globes to prostrate mounds. The degree of "blueness" is extremely variable, although some cultivars can be depended upon to provide reliable color. These include 'Bakeri', 'Copeland', 'Endtz', 'Fat Albert', 'Girard Dwarf', 'Hoopsi', 'Koster', 'Montgomery', 'Moorheim', and 'Thomsen'.* OPPOSITE: *This example of a common juniper is anything but common. Extremely compact and dwarf-growing, the stiffly vertical form of* Juniperus communis *'Compressa' makes a stark contrast to the sprawling, prostrate form of blue Noble fir (*Abies procera *'Glauca Prostata', formerly* Abies nobilis *'Glauca Prostrata').*

FEELING BLUE?

Sometimes you just need a change from green. You may not want to be really daring, just a bit experimental. Blue conifers are just the ticket. Blue adds depth to the landscape, and it combines beautifully with all sorts of colors, especially purple, burgundy, and bronze foliage plants. The blue may vary from just slightly blue-green to robin's egg blue to icy blue-gray. If you plan to have a blue conifer installed by a landscaper, be sure to go out to the nursery and tag the exact tree you want. The color even in a particular species can be extremely variable. It is best to look for specific, named cultivars that have a good reputation in the trade and that exhibit consistent good color. The list below includes a variety of blue conifers cultivars, both dwarf and full size.

Abies concolor (white fir): 'Candicans' (syn. 'Argentea'), 'Compacta', 'Fagerhult', 'Glauca', 'Select Blue', 'Sherwood Blue', 'Violacea'

Abies koreana (Korean fir): 'Blauer Pfiff', 'Blue Standard', 'Horstmann's Silberlocke', 'Silber Mavers', 'Silberzwerg'

Abies lasiocarpa (alpine fir): 'Glauca', 'Glauca Compacta Blue'

Abies nordmanniana (Nordmann fir): 'Glauca', 'Robusta'

Abies procera (noble fir): 'Glauca', 'Nobel', 'Prostrata'

Cedrus deodara (Himalayan cedar): 'Karl Fuchs', 'Prostrate Beauty', 'Sanders Blue'

Cedrus libani ssp.*atlantica* (Atlas cedar): 'Argentea Fastigiata', 'Glauca Pendula', 'Rustic'

Chamaecyparis pisifera (Sawara false cypress): 'Clouded Sky', 'Glauca Nana', 'Murphy Blue'

Cryptomeria japonica (Japanese cedar): 'Elegans Compacta'

Cupressus glabra (smooth-bark cypress): 'Blue Ice', 'Conica'

Juniperus chinensis (Chinese juniper): 'Angelica Blue', 'Blue Cloud' (hybrid), 'Hetzii Glauca', 'Pyramidalis'

Juniperus horizontalis (creeping juniper): 'Argentea', 'Blue Chip', 'Wiltonii'

Juniperus sabina (Savin juniper): 'Blue Forest', 'Mas'

Juniperus scopulorum (rocky mountain juniper): 'Blue Heaven Dwarf', 'Chandler's Silver', 'Kenyonii', 'Salome's Blue', 'Wichita Blue'

Picea englemannii (Engelmann spruce): 'Argentea', 'Compact', 'Vanderwolf's Blue Pyramid'

Picea glauca (white spruce): 'Pendula', 'Sander's Blue'

Picea omorika (Serbian spruce): 'Berliner's Weeper','Expansa', 'Pendula'

Picea pungens (Colorado spruce): 'Bakeri', 'Endtz', 'Fat Albert', 'Globosa', 'Hoopsii', 'Hunnewelliana', 'Ice Blue', 'Pendula', 'Prostrate Blue Mist', 'R.H. Montgomery', 'Thomsen'

Pinus cembra (Swiss stone pine): 'Blue Mound', 'Glauca', 'Silver Sheen'

Pinus flexilis (limber pine): 'Extra Blue', 'Glauca Pendula', 'Glenmore', 'Vanderwolf's Pyramid'

Pinus koraiensis (Korean pine): 'Silveray'

A Touch of Gold

Because conifers keep their needles throughout the seasons, and because the needles provide such dense coverage of the trunk and branches, I tend to think of conifers as structural. They provide a feeling of stability, solidity, and permanence in a garden that changes from week to week. The dark green of yews and Norway spruce so commonly seen could easily make you think of conifers as something dark, sedate, and dull, just what every landscape needs. If that is how you think of conifers, the cultivars listed here should come as a pleasant surprise. Each one displays bright gold coloring (either all year or in at least one season) that will light up the landscape and brighten your outlook. Gold is the perfect partner for almost any green, so plant it with abandon, using it to brighten a display of darker evergreens or in a warm color planting of hostas, grasses, and tall wildflowers.

Abies concolor (white fir): 'Winter Gold'

Abies nordmanniana (Nordmann fir): 'Aureovariegata'

Cedrus deodara (Himalayan cedar): 'Gold Cone', 'Golden Mound', 'Harvest Gold', 'Wells Golden'

Chamaecyparis obtusa (Hinoki false cypress): 'Aurea', 'Fernspray Gold', 'Golden Nymph', 'Goldilocks', 'Lynn's Golden', 'Nana Aurea', 'Nana Lutea', 'Verkade's Sunburst'

Chamaecyparis pisifera (Sawara false cypress): 'Aurea Compacta Nana', 'Bright Gold', 'Filifera Aurea', 'Filifera Sungold', 'Lemon Thread', 'Sulphurea Nana'

Cryptomeria japonica (Japanese cedar): 'Aurea'

Cupressus glabra (smooth-bark cypress): 'Golden Pyramid', 'Sulfurea Aurea'

Juniperus chinensis (Chinese juniper): 'Gold Star', 'Kuriwao Gold', 'Old Gold', 'Plumosa Aurea'

Juniperus communis (common juniper): 'Depressa Aurea', 'Hornibrook's Gold', 'Nana Aurea'

Juniperus horizontalis (creeping juniper): 'Mother Lode' (P.P.#5948)

Juniperus squamata (singleseed juniper): 'Golden Flame'

Juniperus virginiana (Eastern red cedar): 'Plumosa Argentea', 'Sherwoodii'

Larix sibirica (Siberian larch): 'Aurea Magnifica'

Picea mariana (black spruce): 'Aurea'

Picea orientalis (Oriental spruce): 'Aurea Nana', 'Early Gold'

Picea pungens (Colorado spruce): 'Flavescens', 'Stanley Gold'

Pinus cembra (Swiss stone pine): 'Aurea', 'Variegata'

Pinus sylvestris (Scotch pine): 'Gold Medal', 'Nisbet's Gem'

Pseudolarix amabilis (golden larch) (No cultivars available; species color is excellent)

Sciadopitys verticillata (Japanese umbrella pine): 'Aurea', 'Golden Parasol'

Taxus baccata (English yew): 'Dwarf Bright Gold', 'Fastigiata Aurea', 'Linearis', 'Semperaurea'

Taxus cuspidata (Japanese yew): 'Aurea', 'Bright Gold', 'Nana Aurescens'

Thuja occidentalis (American arborvitae): 'Aurea Lane's Gold', 'Cloth of Gold', 'Cristata Aurea', 'Golden Globe', 'Holmstrup Yellow', 'Lutea', 'Watnong Gold'

Tsuga canadensis (Canadian hemlock): 'Aurea Compacta', 'Femii', 'Golden Splendor', 'Lutea', 'New Gold'

ABOVE: ***While it isn't exactly common to see lawns made up entirely of groundcover-type juniper (*****Juniperus*** ***spp.), these prostrate, creeping conifers are especially well-suited to steeply sloped yards or areas that are inaccessible with a mower. Groundhugging junipers are available in shades of blue, green, gold, and variegated forms.***
OPPOSITE: ***A dwarf form of the golden Sawara cypress (*****Chamaecyparis pisifera*** ***'Aurea') adds intrigue to the craggy shelf of this rock garden. The gold-tipped branches seem to pour down the side of the rock like a waterfall. Other plants in this rugged rock garden include species of thyme (*****Thymus*** ***spp.) and catmint (*****Nepeta*** ***spp.).***

ELITE EVERGREENS

Conifers and broadleaf evergreens should be given a prominent position in any landscape with a focus on foliage. Because their leaves and needles are exposed to every weather extreme throughout the year, you may want to spray your evergreens with an antidesiccant in autumn. Broadleaf evergreens such as boxwoods, azaleas, rhododendrons, and some hollies may also perform better if planted in a slightly sheltered location. These precautions should help your evergreens get through the rough weather, especially if they have been watered regularly throughout the year. Keep them stress-free by treating any diseases or insect infestations and fertilizing if necessary.

In return for this minimal maintenance, conifers and broadleaf evergreens add stature and structure to any landscape. Boxwoods (*Buxus* spp.) can be trimmed to create a very low border or a moderate-sized hedge, or may be left to grow as individual specimens. Azaleas and rhododendrons are ideal as understory plants combined with cherries, crabapples, redbuds, or flowering dogwoods for a breathtaking spring show. Deciduous conifers such as the ginkgo (*Ginkgo biloba*), European larch (*Larix decidua*), Japanese larch (*Larix kaempferi*), weeping larch (*Larix* x *pendula*), golden larch (*Pseudolarix amabilis*), and dawn redwood (*Metasequoia glyptostroboides*) bring a whole new look to suburban landscapes, while making interesting conversation pieces, too.

It's hard to beat conifers for form—they range from tiny bonsai trees to completely prostrate rock garden specimens to groundcovers. They can be grown as globes, topiaries, weepers, and creepers, and in shapes from low mounds to mountainous pyramids, from pencil-thin points several feet high to trees spreading 50 feet (15m) wide. Upright, pendulous, conical, columnar, shrubby, or umbrella-shaped —whatever shape you are looking for, you can find it in evergreen form. As if that wasn't enough, the needle evergreens may be soft and silky or stiff and bristly, long and limp or tight and recurved. Foliage may be any shade of green, gray, gold, blue, or white, or variegated. Winter color may turn conifers to gold, russet, purple, or bronze, or to brighter shades of green or gold. Many have beautiful bark and attractive candles and cones.

If you have an eye for form and foliage, look no further. The fun starts here.

BELOW: ***Boxwoods (*****Buxus*** ***spp.) are expensive and fairly slow to establish, but they are perfect for topiary. Have some fun by designing your own topiary shapes—basic "balls" as shown here are easy to shape with just a few snips.***

HOLLY DAYS

Not so long ago, evergreen hollies were something northern gardeners could only dream about. This was frustrating because holly seems such a part of winter holiday decorations, you'd think it would be able to survive cold winters. The problem with a lot of broadleaf evergreens, particularly hollies and boxwoods, is that they suffer from drying winter winds and without protection many will also burn from the sun. Southern gardeners in the past weren't much better off, because many hollies were stressed by extremes of heat and humidity in the South as much as they were stressed by drying winds and winter cold up North.

In the '60s and '70s a new breed of hollies was developed by New York gardener Mrs. F. Leighton Meserve, and additional *Ilex* x *meservae* hybrid blue hollies have been introduced since then. Meserve hollies—like most hollies—need a pollinator in order to produce fruit, so be sure to plant at least one male for up to about ten female hollies. Female meserve hollies include 'Blue Maid', 'Blue Princess', and 'Blue Girl'; males include 'Blue Stallion', 'Blue Prince', and 'Blue Boy'. 'China Girl' and 'China Boy' are more recent meserve hybrids, and they are said to be more cold hardy than the others. A midwestern study indicates that these hollies will perform best when planted in northern exposures.

ABOVE: ***Holly means holidays to many people who live where it thrives. The foliage and berries are used to decorate fireplace mantels, table settings, and doorways, but they are just as pretty in their natural state against a backdrop of snow. Not all hollies have the distinctive shape of the variegated English holly (*****Ilex aquifolium*****) pictured here, but all hollies have ornamental value.***

There are several deciduous hollies, including common winterberry (*Ilex verticillata*), possumhaw (*Ilex decidua*), Japanese winterberry (*Ilex serrata*), and hybrids of the common and Japanese winterberries. To my mind the most attractive foliage and fruits are on those dark green, evergreen, spiny leaves of American holly (*Ilex opaca*), English holly (*Ilex aquifolium*), and Chinese holly (*Ilex cornuta*). Other hollies with spiny foliage are Perny holly (*Ilex pernyi*), Koehne hybrids such as 'Wirt L. Winn', Aquipern holly (*Ilex* x *aquipernyi*), Altaclara (syn. Highclere) holly (*Ilex* x *altaclerensis*), Foster hybrids (*Ilex* x *attenuata*), and hybrids *Ilex* x 'Emily Brunner' and *Ilex* x 'Dr. Kassab'.

Japanese holly (*Ilex crenata*) has small shiny leaves, similar to a littleleaf boxwood and not spiny. Glossy evergreen hollies without spiny foliage include Dahoon holly (*Ilex cassine*), Yaupon holly (*Ilex vomitoria*), lusterleaf holly (*Ilex latifolia*), longstalk holly (*Ilex pedunculosa*), and inkberry (*Ilex glabra*). Whichever type of holly you prefer, make sure it is hardy in your area and plant it where it will get some protection from sun and wind. Hollies have so much to offer in a landscape focusing on foliage, you may want to start your own collection.

CHAPTER 7

Variegated Foliage

VARIEGATED FOLIAGE—LEAVES THAT ARE NOT ALL ONE COLOR, BUT EDGED, STRIPED, MOTTLED, OR OTHERWISE COMBINED ON A SINGLE LEAF—CAN BE A TOUCHY SUBJECT. WHEN IT COMES TO VARIEGATED PLANTS, IT SEEMS THAT MOST GARDENERS EITHER LOVE THEM OR HATE THEM. THEIR SUPPORTERS PRAISE THE DISTINCTIVE MARKINGS AND NOTE HOW THE LIGHTER COLORATION HELPS BRIGHTEN THE WHOLE PLANT. DETRACTORS CLAIM THAT VARIEGATION DISTRACTS OR CLASHES WITH FLOWERS, AND MAKES IT VERY DIFFICULT TO SITE THE PLANT SO IT IS AESTHETICALLY PLEASING.

While sage is a standard in herb gardens, this portrait of tricolor sage (*Salvia officinalis *'Tricolor') demonstrates why this hardy herb deserves a place in the perennial garden too.

I find myself hovering on the fence, sometimes leaning towards variegation, sometimes against. When I first became obsessed with gardening, I sought out variegated iris, variegated obedient plant, variegated redtwig dogwood, variegated box elder, and any number of other variegated plants. I was fascinated with plants that had something different to offer, either in foliage or in flower. As I watched these plants grow, I came to the sensible conclusion that different is not necessarily better. The variegated redtwig dogwood, for instance, seemed like a great idea in theory, but most specimens I have seen have thin, rather tatty leaves that look sickly instead of sublime.

On the other hand, some variegated plants look fantastic—take *Hydrangea macrophylla* 'Variegata Mariesii', for example. Variegated hostas don't seem to bother anyone, and I have never had a problem siting them in a suitable place. The five-leaf aralia (*Acanthopanax sieboldianus* 'Variegatus') is stunning in variegated form, as is Japanese angelica (*Aralia elata* 'Aureovariegata') and the variegated giant dogwood (*Cornus controversa* 'Variegata'). I like variegated weigela as much as I like any weigela, which means sometimes I do, sometimes I don't.

Fans of variegated plants should be thrilled because there has never been so much to choose from. If you've always hated variegated plants, remember—there's an exception to every rule. New variegated plants are being introduced all the time, and you may just find something you'll love.

RIGHT: ***Hostas, such as those pictured here, are great examples of variegated plants because they exhibit so many different forms of variegation—they also come in an incredibly large number of colors, color combinations, leaf textures, leaf sizes, flower sizes, forms, and varying degrees of fragrance. Hostas are often seen lined up in a row along the sides of suburban houses. It would be a lot more interesting and artistic to mix hostas with different types of variegation, or to make a "hosta garden" with the large-leaved varieties at the back and the edging-type hostas at the front of the border.***

Using Light and Shadow

When the emphasis in a garden is on form and foliage, it can be useful to accent these features by manipulating light and shadow. Make the most of natural light by observing which parts of your garden are highlighted by the early morning and late afternoon sun. Tall grasses and "see-through" plants like baby's breath and Russian sage look breathtaking with the sun shining through them. Set a floodlight in front of or behind these plants for a dramatic nighttime effect.

Use visual tricks like mirrors to make your garden seem to have more depth. Fix a mirror to a fence or wall or place a gazing globe among the flowers. The reflective qualities of a honeylocust hanging over a still, sunlit pond adds to the pond's impact—any tree with filtered shade and small leaves will do. Fix floodlights in the upper branches of the tree so they will shine down through the tree at night; alternately, aim one floodlight up into the tree to highlight its leaves and branches.

Flickering torches are evocative but probably a little risky for most gardens; tiny white fairy lights can add a magical touch in a safer manner. Larger landscape lighting fixtures can be disguised by large-leaved plants such as hostas, or fixed in the branches of trees. Weeping trees or trees with strong architectural features can be used to dramatic effect with lighting either aimed directly into the tree's branches or at an angle that will cast shadows against a nearby wall.

Landscape lighting is an art—downlighting, uplighting, moonlighting, accent lighting, diffused lighting, silhouetting, cross-lighting, grazing, and shadowing are just a few of the available techniques. For more complicated patterns of light and shadow, have a lighting specialist set up a network of lights to make the most of your plants and structures. Inexpensive low-voltage systems are easy to install but are limited as to their usefulness. Line voltage lighting is at the other end of the spectrum, and in most states must be installed by licensed electricians. In between these two extremes, a wide variety of landscape lighting can be found, with a wide spectrum of price and adaptability.

Light and shadow are often neglected in landscape design. Make the most of these features to create an extra dimension of interest in your garden.

ABOVE: *The Nanking cherry (*Prunus tomentosa*), sometimes called Manchu cherry, is a popular landscape tree for several reasons: it has edible fruit, ornamental bark, spring flowers, and a broad-growing, interesting habit. It performs best in full sun, so take advantage of that characteristic by positioning the tree where the sun will use its artistry to highlight the foliage, as in the scene above.*
OPPOSITE: *The play of light and shadow on the straplike leaves of this variegated giant reed (*Arundo donax *'Versicolor') makes each detail come into prominence. Create your own magic with landscape lighting or take advantage of natural sunlight by positioning plants so that the sun will backlight or filter through their leaves.*

Variegated Plants of All Kinds

Variegated plants must sell well, because they are being produced and sold in large numbers. No matter what type of plant you are looking for, you can probably find it in a variegated form. The list here is by no means comprehensive, but it will give you a good idea of what's available.

BELOW: ***Cannas have been around a long time but they have recently been "discovered" by gardeners and landscape designers. Few plants can match their bold flowers, but equally important for design purposes are a canna's massive leaves. Many cultivars have variegated foliage, such as 'Pretoria' (Canna × hortensis 'Pretoria'), shown here in an inspired plant combination with colorful lantanas.***

ANNUALS

Canna × 'Striped Beauty', 'Striata' (canna)

Lunaria annua 'Alba Variegata' (honesty)

Phormium tenax 'Sundowner' (New Zealand flax)

Tropaeolum majus 'Alaska' (nasturtium)

Vinca major 'Variegata' (annual vinca)

PERENNIALS

Astrantia major 'Sunningdale Variegated' (astrantia)

Euphorbia marginata (syn. *Euphorbia variegata*, snow-on-the-mountain)

Hosta 'Wide Brim', 'Shogun', 'Geisha', 'Whirlwind', 'Masquerade', etc. (hosta)

Hosta undulata var. *univittata* (hosta)

Phlox × 'Norah Leigh' (phlox)

Phystostegia virginianum var. *nana* 'Variegata'(obedient plant)

Polygonatum odoratum var. *thunbergii* 'Variegatum' (Solomon's seal)

Pulmonaria saccharata 'Little Star' (lungwort)

Viola variegata (variegated violet)

GROUNDCOVERS AND BULBS

Ajuga spp., most cultivars (bugleweed)

Arum italicum 'Marmoratum' (arum)

Fritillaria imperialis 'Variegata' (crown imperial)

Hedera colchica 'Dentata Variegata', 'Sulphur Heart' (ivy)

Iris pallida 'Variegata' (orris root)

Pachysandra terminalis 'Variegata' (Japanese spurge)

Vinca minor 'Ralph Shugert', 'Sterling Silver', 'Aureovariegata' (perennial vinca, periwinkle)

TOP: ***Few plants can compare with the crown imperial (*****Fritillaria imperialis*****) for interesting form and flowers. Add variegation, and you have a plant that will draw comments from every visitor to your garden. The bulbs are available in red and yellow flowering varieties; pictured here is the red-flowering cultivar 'Variegata'.*** BOTTOM: ***Nasturtiums (*****Tropaeolum majus*****) have been popular with gardeners for many years, and with good reason. They are colorful climbers, look interesting in containers or planting beds, are easy to grow, and are even edible. The cultivar 'Alaska', shown here, has the added attraction of an interesting pattern of variegated foliage.***

GRASSES AND REEDS

Acorus calamus 'Variegatus' (sweet flag)

Arundo donax 'Versicolor' (striped giant reed)

Carex morrowii 'Variegata' (Japanese sedge)

Cortaderia selloana 'Gold Band' (pampas grass)

Miscanthus sinensis 'Malepartus', 'Variegatus' (Japanese silver grass)

Molina caerulea ssp. *caerula* 'Variegata' (Moor grass)

Phalaris arundinacea 'Luteo-Picta' (golden ribbon grass)

HERBS

Brassica variegata (variegated mustard)

Mentha × *gracilis* 'Variegata' (ginger mint)

Melissa officinalis 'Variegata' (lemon balm)

Salvia officinalis 'Iceterina', 'Tricolor' (common sage)

Symphytum officinale 'Variegatum' (comfrey)

SHRUBS

Abutilon pictum 'Gold Dust' (abutilon)

Acanthopanax sieboldiana 'Variegatus' (five-leaf aralia)

Aralia elata 'Aureovariegata' (Japanese angelica)

Aucuba japonica 'Variegata' (Japanese laurel)

Buddleia davidii 'Harlequin' (butterfly bush)

Berberis thunbergii 'Rose Glow' (Japanese barberry)

Buxus sempervirens 'Elegantissima' (silver boxwood)

Cornus alba 'Elegantissima' (Tatarian dogwood)

LEFT: ***Many grasses and reeds are available in variegated cultivars; shown here is a border of variegated sweet flag (*****Acorus calamus*** ***'Variegatus'). It's difficult to find an ornamental grass that doesn't look good, but the variegated grasses seem to be especially eye-catching when they are situated so the sun can shine through and highlight each blade.*** ABOVE: ***Most gardeners either love or hate variegated foliage—it can be difficult to work into a design, but when carefully placed the plants can be breathtaking. The variegated mock orange (*****Philadelphus coronarius*** ***'Variegata') pictured here is set off by hybrid lupines (*****Lupinus ×*** ***'Band of Nobles').***

SHRUBS (CONTINUED)

Cornus sericea 'Silver and Gold' (red osier dogwood)

Cotoneaster horizontalis 'Variegatus' (creeping cotoneaster)

Daphne × 'Briggs Moonlight' (daphne)

Eleaganus pungens 'Hosoba-Fukurin', also 'Variegata' (Russian olive)

Euonymus fortunei 'Emerald and Gold', 'Emerald Gaiety' (euonymus)

Hibiscus syriacus 'Purpureus Variegatus' (rose-of-sharon)

Hydrangea macrophylla 'Variegata Mariesii' (bigleaf hydrangea)

Hypericum × *moseranum* 'Tricolor' (St. John's wort)

Ilex × *altaclarensis* 'Golden King', 'Lawsoniana' (Altaclara or highclere holly)

Kerria japonica 'Picta' (Japanese kerria)

Ligustrum lucidum 'Tricolor' (Chinese privet)

Ligustrum ovalifolium 'Argenteum' (California privet)

Philadelphus coronarius 'Variegata' (sweet mock-orange)

Pieris japonica 'Variegata' (Japanese andromeda)

Pittosporum tenuifolium 'Silver Queen' (pittosporum)

Rhamnus alaterna 'Argenteovariegata' (buckthorn)

Symphoricarpos orbiculatus 'Variegatus' (snowberry)

Weigela florida 'Variegata', 'Albo-variegata' (old-fashioned weigela)

LEFT: ***The sunny foliage of 'Emerald 'n' Gold' euonymus (*****Euonymus fortunei*** ***'Emerald 'n' Gold') adds as much interest to the garden as the dazzling fuchsias hanging over the birdbath. This species of euonymus is available in a wide range of variegated cultivars, including 'Emerald Gaiety', 'Harlequin', and 'Silver Gem'.***

TREES

Acer negundo 'Elegans', 'Flamingo' (box elder)

Acer palmatum 'Butterfly', 'Ukigumo', 'Dissectum Variegatum' (Japanese maple)

Acer platanoides 'Drummondii' (Norway maple)

Acer pseudoplatanus 'Leopoldii' (sycamore maple)

Cornus alternifolia 'Argentea' (pagoda dogwood)

Cornus controversa 'Variegata' (giant dogwood)

Cornus florida 'Rainbow' (flowering dogwood)

Cornus florida 'Tricolor' (flowering dogwood)

Cornus mas 'Variegata' (corneliancherry dogwood)

Fagus sylvatica 'Roseomarginata' (European beech)

Ilex aquifolium 'Argentea Marginata', 'Ferox Argentea' (English holly)

Liriodendron tulipifera 'Aureomarginatum' (tuliptree)

Populus × *jackii* 'Gileadensis', syn. *P.* × candicans 'Aurora' (balsam poplar of Gilead)

Sambucus nigra 'Albovariegata' (elder)

ABOVE: ***Although this young specimen of variegated dogwood (*Cornus controversa *'Variegata') appears dwarfed by the richly colored foliage at its base, it will eventually reach nearly 50 feet (15m) in height with strongly horizontal branching.***

CHAPTER 8

Foliage Plants with a Purpose

Foliage that is ornamental adds an important element to any garden, but some foliage plants also serve a useful purpose. Plants that are fragrant help to soothe our stressed psyches, and if they are ornamental, too, so much the better. Fruits and vegetables are no longer the second-class citizens of the gardening world, as newer and more colorful cultivars abound. Even old faithfuls are finding their way into mixed planting beds. Herbs are useful on three levels: culinary, ornamental, and medicinal.

*Many forms of basil are suitable both for the herb garden and the perennial border. Here the rich color and distinctive form of 'Purple Ruffles' basil (*Ocimum basilicum *'Purple Ruffles') is an excellent foil for the sunny foliage of golden feverfew (*Tanacetum parthenium *var.* aureum*).*

When you have limited time and space for gardening, as most people do, it makes sense to incorporate plants that serve more than one purpose. Chives are highly ornamental, but you can also snip off a few to add zing to your dinner instead of just admiring the way they look. Blueberry bushes are beautiful in spring, summer, and autumn, while the blueberries are so tasty you will have to beat the birds to them. Alpine strawberries have become an accepted part of the perennial border, and now ornamental cabbage and kale have become staples of any autumn planting.

As water gardens gain popularity, gardeners are moving away from formal ponds and discovering the joys of more natural water gardens and ponds. By surrounding the pond with greenery it not only stays healthy, but you can also attract birds and wildlife and often feed the fish, too. Be cautious with plant selection, though, because some plants defeat the object by spreading so densely that they literally suffocate pond life.

No matter what type of garden you are creating, be sure to look beyond the flowers. Foliage can be fantastic, fascinating, and fun. But practical, too? Who could ask for more?

ABOVE: ***One of the reasons for the growing interest in herbs is their many uses in the garden—in the kitchen garden or perennial border, or for medicinal, culinary, or purely ornamental use. Although a few herbs have pretty flowers, in most cases foliage is the main attraction, as in the golden lemon balm (*Melissa officinalis* 'Aurea'). Planted near a path this showy herb gives off its signature lemony scent when the leaves are brushed by passersby.*** OPPOSITE: ***A vegetable garden can be accented with perennials or other nonedible plants, such as the assortment of coleus shown here. Some gardeners even incorporate ornamental vegetables directly into perennial beds and borders.***

FRAGRANT PLANTS

Aromatherapy is big business these days—just look at all the stores selling candles, aromatic oils, incense, room sprays, dried flower potpourris, scented bath soaps, and shampoos, not to mention countless aftershaves and colognes. The idea that fragrance can be used to relieve stress is nothing new; manufacturers have just gotten better at packaging it. Still, there's nothing like the real thing—walking into a garden and inhaling deeply to absorb all the fragrances in the air.

Whether it is the smell of rain on fallen leaves or the hot sun on new-mown grass, there is always some kind of fragrance in the garden. The most pleasure-filled fragrances come from individual plants—their flowers, their foliage, sometimes even their stems. In some cases all you have to do to enjoy the fragrance is to put your nose by the flower and breathe in. Other plants don't release their fragrance until you brush against them or rub your fingers over the leaves. In either case, it makes sense to install scented plants where their fragrance can be easily noticed and enjoyed.

ABOVE: ***The California incense cedar (*****Calocedrus decurrens*****, formerly* **Libocedrus decurrens*****) is native to the West Coast but has proven to be adaptable in regions all across the continent. It performs best in soils that are moist but well-drained and fairly acidic. The bark and foliage are very attractive, and its conical shape would make it an elegant addition to a formal landscape.*** OPPOSITE: ***Rose-scented geraniums (*****Pelargonium graveolens*****) and other scented geraniums bear small flowers, but their true attraction is their incomparably fragrant foliage.***

There are endless variations on a scented theme, and determining which fragrant plants give you the most enjoyment is a purely personal thing. In nature, a scent may be overpowering or so light that it teases the senses. It can be sweet or spicy, citrusy or musky, subtle or strong. Try to experience a fragrant plant before assuring it a place in your garden—what sounds great on paper might be unpleasant up close.

Even though this book is focusing on foliage, I am including some plants with fragrant flowers in the following plant list. Not because their flowers are ornamental—although in many cases, they are—but because their fragrance compels you to take notice of other details in the garden besides those that are blatantly visual. To fully enjoy a garden, you need to notice every tiny detail, not just the flowers. In this case, the best way to appreciate fragrance is to close your eyes and inhale.

Calocedrus decurrens (incense cedar)
Calycanthus floridus (Carolina allspice)
Chimonanthus praecox (wintersweet)
Clematis montana var. *rubens* (anemone clematis)
Clethra alnifolia (summersweet)
Convallaria majalis (lily-of-the-valley)
Daphne × *burkwoodii* (Burkwood daphne)
Daphne cneorum (garland flower)
Dianthus spp. (pinks, carnations)
Galium odoratum (sweet woodruff)
Gladiolus tristis (fragrant gladiola)
Hamamelis mollis (Chinese witchhazel)
Heliotropium arborescens (heliotrope)
Hemerocallis × 'Hyperion' ('Hyperion' daylily)
Hosta × 'Royal Standard'
Hyacinthus spp. (hyacinth)
Iris × *germanica* (old bearded iris hybrids)
Iris reticulata (reticulated iris)
Itea virginica (Virginia sweetspire)
Jasminum spp. (jasmine)
Lavandula spp. (lavender)
Lilium regale (regal lily, and many other *Lilium* spp.)
Lindera benzoin (spicebush)
Lonicera spp. (honeysuckle)
Magnolia grandiflora (evergreen magnolia)
Malus sargentii (Sargent crabapple)
Malus × 'Satin Cloud' ('Satin Cloud' crabapple)
Matthiola bicornis (night-scented stock)
Melissa officinalis (lemon balm)
Mentha spp. (mints)
Myrrhis odorata (sweet cicely)
Myrtus communis (myrtle)
Narcissus jonquilla (jonquil)
Narcissus poeticus (narcissus)
Nicotiana spp. (flowering tobacco)
Nymphaea odorata (water lily)
Ocimum basilicum (basil)
Oxydendron arboreum (sourwood)
Pelargonium graveolens (rose-scented geranium, and other *Pelargonium* spp.)
Philadelphus spp. (mock orange)
Polianthes tuberosa (tuberose)
Rhododendron arborescens (sweet azalea)
Rosa damascena (damask rose)
Rosa gallica (Provence rose)
Rosmarinus officinalis (rosemary)
Syringa spp. (lilac)
Thymus spp. (thyme)
Viburnum × *burkwoodii* 'Mohawk' ('Mohawk' viburnum)
Viburnum carlesii (Koreanspice viburnum)
Viburnum × *juddii* (Judd viburnum)
Viola odorata (violet)

HERBAL DELIGHTS

ABOVE: ***Spearmint (*****Mentha spicata*****) has many uses in addition to its strictly ornamental value in the garden. Like peppermint and applemint, spearmint can be used in tea or vinegar and as flavorings in sauces, desserts, and vegetable dishes. Aromatic oils from these mints are also used in soap, drink, toothpaste, medicine, and candy, just to name a few. All types of mints will spread rapidly and are best restrained in a large container.*** OPPOSITE TOP: ***Rosemary (*****Rosmarinus officinalis*****) grows as a woody shrub in warmer climates, but it is not hardy in colder regions. This ornamental herb has culinary value and is also popular as a topiary subject.*** OPPOSITE BOTTOM: ***Sweet cicely (*****Myrrhis odorata*****) has lacy, fernlike foliage, and grows well in damp, shady spots, an unusual trait for herbs.***

Herbs grow on you. When I started dabbling in herbs a few years ago, I really had no knowledge of herb gardening beyond the standard plants: mint, chives, and lavender. Shortly after moving to Cincinnati, I attended an herb fair and decided to take a chance with tansy, tarragon, marjoram, oregano, and thyme. I planted the tansy and tarragon in a large wooden barrel already planted with nasturtiums and chives. I have mixed feelings about the tansy, since I have discovered it spreads like the dickens and gets a little too tall and bushy even for my large container. The trouble is, I wouldn't dare plant it outside of a container knowing how it spreads. The flowers are very attractive, though, so I leave it alone until it gets straggly, and then I cut it back sharply. That first winter broke all kinds of records for cold, so I was very surprised to find the tarragon back the next year. The foliage is pretty but, in my container at least, it is hardy but not vigorous. The marjoram and oregano went into another wooden barrel stocked with mint and, in the summer, 'Blueberry Cheesecake' gladioli and 'Purple Wave' petunias. The tiny leaves spill over the sides of the barrel, while the mint covers the gladiolus stalks in between flowering. (Hummingbirds love this combination!)

Thyme is to blame for my current addiction to herbs, though. I planted one tiny plant of creeping thyme and another of Mother-of-thyme. The latter

basil, borage, feverfew, hyssop, bergamot, coriander, Corsican mint, winter savory, rue, more kinds of thyme, more kinds of lavender, even more sage, dill, fennel, lemon verbena, lovage, musk mallow, marsh mallow, santolina, saffron crocus, angelica, and probably others that have slipped my mind.

The fragrance of many of these herbs is wonderful. In some cases the flowers are very ornamental, but the foliage is almost always attractive and interesting. If you have never planted herbs, start with something simple like lavender, thyme, or purple sage. Once you've tried purple sage, you'll be curious about tricolor sage. And after that you'll just have to plant pineapple sage. By the time you have entire planting beds filled with different species of lavender, thyme, and sage, it will be too late—you'll be hooked on herbs.

is healthy and attractive, but the creeping thyme now fills more than 2 square feet. In the summer it is alive with bees, even during a year where scientists announced a critical shortage of bees nationwide. The bees were far too busy to bother anyone, even though the thyme is planted next to a well-traveled walk. Flowering, fragrant, with delicate foliage—creeping thyme has become one of my favorite plants.

Since then I have experimented with salad burnet, lemon balm, Roman and German chamomile, many kinds of sage, several mints, at least ten scented geraniums a year, more varieties of garlic and chives, catmint, catnip, lots of

LEFT: ***This sunny garden contains an interesting mix of foliage plants, including feathertop (*****Pennisetum villosum*****), wormwood (*****Artemisia*** ***spp.), barberry (*****Berberis*** ***spp.), and yucca.*** ABOVE: ***Many varieties of thyme (*****Thymus*** ***spp.) are available—enough to make it possible to plant a garden entirely of different thyme species. Thyme is often grown between paving stones because it is able to withstand some foot traffic, and releases its fragrance with each step.***

Vegetables Have Foliage, Too

Many landscapes have strictly regimented layouts: this section is for roses, this one is for perennials, this area is for annuals, this bed for herbs and, hidden away someplace, there is usually a plot for vegetables. Gradually, gardeners are coming to realize the benefits of blending shrub roses in mixed beds, and planting perennials with annuals and herbs in flower borders. Fruiting shrubs and perennial strawberries are accepted as equals in an ornamental garden but, for the most part, vegetables are still hidden away like poor relations.

There are exceptions—hyacinth bean, scarlet runner bean, and other climbers are becoming more common in mixed garden areas, while ornamental cabbage and kale are now considered companion plants to chrysanthemums. But there are many more vegetables that have attractive—even stunning—foliage, and these should not be neglected. Artichokes are related to an interesting perennial called cardoon (*Cynara cardunculus*), but they have the added benefit of being edible. Chili peppers are extremely ornamental—here in Cincinnati, there is even a chili pepper club promoting their benefits in the garden. Ornamental onions and garlic can easily be worked into a perennial bed.

Rhubarb, chard, 'Nagaoke' Chinese cabbage, bok choy, 'Red Giant' and 'Osaka' Japanese mustard greens, 'Red Velvet' okra, 'Malabar' spinach, 'Petite Rouge' ornamental lettuce, radicchio, winter purslane, parsley—all of these offer unusual and attractive foliage that you can also serve with dinner. It seems a shame if they are only used for salads, though, since many leafy vegetables look attractive for a long period. Some vegetables look interesting as they grow, such as brussels sprouts, ornamental eggplant, and purple kohlrabi, particularly the cultivar 'Early Purple Vienna'. Experiment with these and other vegetables in your herb bed or perennial border—then smile and look mysterious when your gardening friends say, "What is that incredible plant?"

ABOVE: ***Some vegetables are just too pretty to hide in the vegetable garden. The Swiss chard cultivar 'Rainbow' pictured here not only adds color to a summer feast, it also turns a vegetable bed into a work of art.*** OPPOSITE: ***Even a simple planting of cabbage, lettuce, and strawberries can be eye-catching and ornamental. Make your vegetable garden a focal point by adding bean-pole teepees covered in colorful scarlet runner beans or towers of exotic-looking Malabar spinach.***

Foliage Plants for Water Gardens

The first plant that most people associate with water gardens is probably the water lily—it has wonderful foliage, but most people choose it for their water gardens because of the beautiful flowers. There is no disputing that the sight of a lotus or water lily floating above the water is memorable, but there are many foliage plants that make an equally unforgettable picture when planted in or around a pond or water garden. Some green plants have the added benefit of oxygenating the water, while others provide food for fish—sometimes much to the gardener's dismay. In some cases water-loving plants will spread into large clumps, so it may be better to select more contained plants if your water garden is small.

It would be easy to fill a book with water-loving plants, their characteristics, planting requirements, and growing needs. This list is just a starting point for those who are looking for attractive foliage plants to accent their water garden or pond; some listed plants also have decorative flowers.

Acorus calamus and other *Acorus* spp. (sweet flag)
Arisaema triphyllum (Jack-in-the-pulpit)
Athyrium pycnocarpon (glade fern)
Carex spp. (sedge)
Elodea canadensis (elodea)
Gunnera manicata (giant rhubarb)
Larix laricina (larch)
Lindera benzoin (spicebush)
Matteucia struthiopteris (ostrich fern)
Nasturtium officinale (watercress)
Peltandra virginica (arrow arum)
Peltiphyllum peltatum (umbrella plant)
Pistia stratiotes (water lettuce)
Pontederia cordata (pickerel rush)
Rodgersia pinnata (rodgersia)
Sagittaria latifolia (arrowhead)
Thelypteris palustris (marsh fern)
Vaccinium macrocarpon (cranberry)
Xyris iridfolia (yellow-eyed grass)

RIGHT: ***The upright leaves of pickerel rush (*****Pontederia cordata*****) seem to be reaching out of the water and up towards the sun in this attractive water garden. This versatile plant will grow either in boggy soil or with its roots covered by as much as 12 inches (30cm) of water. Note that pickerel rush can be invasive, so you may wish to confine it to a submerged pot.***

RIGHT: ***Rodgersia*** **(Rodgersia *spp.)* has large, lustrous leaves that may scorch easily in strong sun. Make sure to grow this plant in the light shade and boggy soil it likes best, and mix it with other moisture-loving plants such as hostas, Japanese coltsfoot, and irises.**

OPPOSITE: ***Water lilies*** **(Nymphaea *spp.)* are the most easily recognized and probably the most popular of all plants for the water garden. Although the flowers are undeniably beautiful, the leaves have an elegant simplicity that is beautiful in its own way.**

RIGHT: ***This mass planting of variegated Dalmatian iris (*Iris pallida* 'Variegata') will be equally effective after the flowers have faded. The foliage stays crisp and colorful for several months, and while in bloom the flowers bring the added benefit of fragrance.***

Chapter 9

Weird and Wonderful

There are all kinds of words to describe foliage plants, but a few almost defy description. Yews usually blend in with the landscape, but when they have been sheared into topiary forms they can become something otherworldly. There are hostas that gardeners describe as "huge," but they pale against the massive leaves of great gunnera and the castor bean. From tiny baby's toes to strange houseplants like the staghorn fern, nature abounds with weirdness.

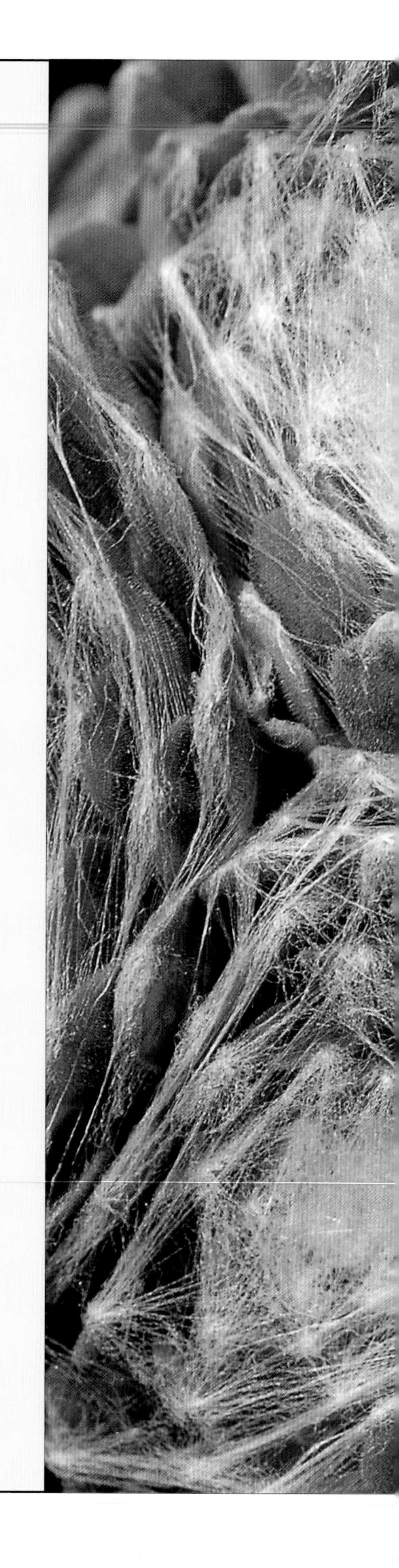

The botanical name for this species of houseleek (**Sempervivum arachnoideum*****) uses the Latin term for the spider family—Arachnid—to indicate that the plant "resembles spiders," or, in this case, the spider's web or cobweb.***

This chapter takes a brief look at the weirdness of nature. Be delicate and call them "unusual" or "strange" but even the familiar artichoke could safely be called "bizarre." These plants differ from the usual landscape plants by their size, shape, or scent, or by their spiky leaves or strange needles. In some cases, plants are trained into weirdness through arts of bonsai or topiary. Individual plants may attain weirdness through storm damage, erosion, or sheer age. Many forms of cactus and succulents appear strange in comparison with more familiar plants, while tropicals and antipodean plants can still leave us staring in wonderment.

Who wants plants in their landscape to be called weird? Some gardeners actually collect weird plants, while others study them. Topiary and bonsai are used by some to stamp their individuality on a specific plant, instead of on the garden as a whole. Since many gardeners pride themselves on their knowledge of plants, it can be fun to stump the experts with rarities. (Just don't admit that you were stumped first!) Some of these plants can be found easily, while others may require a search of public gardens or specialty mail-order nurseries. Think of it as a kind of scavenger hunt for weird and wonderful treasures.

RIGHT: ***Australian sundew (*****Drocera binata*****) has sticky leaves that help it trap and digest insects. It is a short-lived plant and notoriously difficult to grow, requiring regular applications of rainwater and, of course, flies and other insects.***

ABOVE: *Like the Australian sundew, the hooded pitcher plant (*Darlingtonia californica*) is an insectivore. The hooded pitcher looks uncannily like a snake's head, while the unusual "forked tongue" of the plant adds to the eerie effect and explains one of its common names—cobra plant.*

FREAK SHOW

Foliage gardens can be fun, if you want to dabble in plants that are a little, well, bizarre. Weird-looking plants come in all different shapes and sizes, from tiny rock garden plants to huge trees. There are many weird and wonderful plants among the cactus and succulent varieties. Take sedums, for instance, which produce not only the familiar 'Dragon's Blood' groundcover but also strange houseplants called jelly bean sedum (*Sedum pachyphyllum*) and donkey's tail (*S. morganianum*). Other unusual succulents include cobweb houseleek (*Sempervivum arachnoideum*), tiger jaws faucaria (*Faucaria tigrina*), and string of beads senecio (*Senecio rowleyanus*).

Because many of the plants we consider strange originate in tropical climates, North American gardeners may need to pamper theirs indoors, in a greenhouse, or a combination of indoor/outdoor conditions, taking advantage of sultry summer weather. Pamper the following plants, but do it carefully: Venus fly trap (*Dionaea muscipula*), pitcher plants (*Darlingtonia californica*, *Nepenthes coccinea,* and *Sarracenia* spp.), sticky-leaved plants such as Australian sundew (*Drosera binata*), and spiky-leaved plants such as the century plant (*Agave americana*.)

Two ferns are unlike most people's idea of a fern—the staghorn fern (*Platycerium bifurcatum*, syn. *P. alcicome*)

OPPOSITE: ***The staghorn fern (*****Platycerium bifurcatum*****) looks as much like a moosehead with green antlers as it does a plant. The larger leaves of Regal elkhorn fern (*****Platycerium grande*****) display the same effect, only more so.*** BELOW: ***Many unusual plants belong to the sedum genus, including the donkey's tail sedum (*****Sedum morganianum*****) shown here. Because the succulent leaves of this species have a trailing habit, it is often used in hanging baskets.*** RIGHT: ***A mature, healthy specimen of staghorn fern (*****Platycerium bifurcatum*****) holds pride of place in this outdoor setting.***

and the regal elkhorn fern (*Platycerium grande*). When it comes to cactus, almost every plant has a certain weirdness, but none more so than the brain cactus (*Echinofossulocactus zacatecasensis*), goat's horn cactus (*Astrophytum capricorne*), and chain cactus (*Rhipsalis paradoxa*).

Bizarre plants sneak into our vegetable beds and herb gardens, too—consider the rhubarb, artichoke, brussel sprout, kohlrabi, and globe thistle. Love-lies-bleeding (*Amaranthus caudatus*) is an old-fashioned flower that looks as strange as its name, while the cocks-comb celosia (*Celosia cristata*) hardly looks real at all. The castor bean plant (*Ricinus communis*) is one of nature's giants, but beware, it is poisonous. Two perennials are also known for their huge leaves—great gunnera (*Gunnera manicata*) and (*Darmera peltata*, formerly *Peltiphyllum peltatum*); both perform best in wet sites. The mouse arum (*Arisarum proboscideum*) and the voodoo lily (*Sauromatum venosum*) are freaky enough for anyone, while the cushion shaped mounds of *Erigeron pulcellus* 'Meadow Muffin' would barely fit in a button hole.

Be bold, be daring, be a little freaky. Try something completely different in your garden this year.

Poisonous Plants

Poisonous plants have their place in nature, but gardeners with allergies or young children must be cautious about inviting any of these plants into their landscapes. Poison ivy (*Toxicodendron radicans*, formerly *Rhus radicans*) is the best known of North American poisonous plants, although not many people can actually pick it out on a walk in the woods. The old saying "leaflets three, let it be" doesn't take into consideration two important details: first, poison ivy doesn't always have three leaflets (some varieties have many more, and some plants have assorted numbers of leaflets on an individual specimen), and second, many other plants do have "leaflets three" and if you don't know what you're looking for, this can be extremely confusing. In the autumn, look for three leaves that have a brief flush of beautiful red-gold autumn color. Most of the time I find it easier to watch for the distinctive vines, which look as if they have been attached to the tree (or fence, or shed, or anything) with millions of hairy tendrils. Be extremely careful when dealing with poison ivy—all parts are toxic, any time of year.

Poison sumac (*Toxicodendron vernix*), sometimes mistakenly called poison dogwood or poison elder, looks similar to the nontoxic smooth sumac (*Rhus glabra*)—if it has red fruits it is the safe sumac, if it has white bunches of fruits and drupes, that is the poisonous variety. Poison oak (*Toxicodendron diversilobum*) is also very common, and it sometimes looks a lot like poison ivy, except that its leaves and fruits are fuzzy while poison ivy is not. The leaves of poison oak, like poison ivy, can be extremely variable, but they often have shapes similar to regular oak leaves.

There are two types of poisonous plants—those that are poisonous to touch and those that are poisonous to ingest. Because many of these plants go by regional common names, gardeners with young children are best advised to contact their local poison center to find out which plants in your area should be avoided.

ABOVE: ***Nature doesn't always distinguish between beauty and the beastly. This breathtaking leaf is from a plant that should be admired from a safe distance—it is called poison oak (*****Toxicodendron diversilobum*****, formerly *****Rhus diversiloba*****). Poison ivy (*****Toxicodendron radicans*****, formerly *****Rhus radicans*****) has great autumn color, too.***
OPPOSITE: ***The castor oil plant (*****Ricinus communis*****) has fabulous foliage and reaches the height of a small tree, but the beans are deadly—a single bean can kill.***

TOPIARY PLANTS

Topiary, the art of sculpting or training plants into specific, artificial shapes, is an ancient art that has waxed and waned in popularity over the centuries. It may seem at odds with modern trends towards natural, native landscaping, but topiary is enjoying a surge of popularity. Many people are bringing topiary into the home, in small containers on tiny wire frames. Others are trained as standards or set in large outdoor containers. On a large scale, topiary is best suited to formal gardens or gardens with a medieval theme such as a knot garden.

The most common trimmed or sheared topiaries are probably boxwood and yew, although ivy is used most often in smaller, trained topiaries. Bedding geraniums and scented geraniums are sometimes trained as tall standards or on topiary frames, as is rosemary. Small, sheared topiaries are sometimes created from junipers or the tightly formed dwarf Alberta spruce. Citrus trees, heliotrope, bay

LEFT: ***This is topiary in one of its most traditional forms. Many plants that are grafted onto "standards" can be pruned in topiary form, although the most commonly used plants are probably boxwood, bay laurel, juniper, rosemary, rose, yew, or lavender cotton.***

laurel, lavender cotton, bougainvillea, lavender, sage, lantanas, miniature roses, fuchsias, rosemary, and small-leaved azaleas can also be trimmed and trained to some extent.

Topiary involves a little more work than some gardeners want to take on, and it is not the kind of work that is often tackled by landscape contractors or maintenance crews. Especially when the plants are young, it is important that they are trained, tied, and trimmed until they begin to conform to the desired shape. Because they are often containerized, it is important to establish a regular regime of watering and fertilizing, at the same time keeping an eye out for any insect infestations or disease problems. There are several excellent books that describe step-by-step what is required to create the topiary your heart desires. Topiary is not for everyone—or every garden—but in the right place, a topiary that has been well designed and cared for can be as attractive and eye-catching as any garden sculpture.

RIGHT: ***Topiary can be used to enhance a formal garden or to add a touch of humor to the landscape. The example here is created out of boxwood, but other plant materials can also make effective topiaries. To see lots of topiary examples taken to their "goofiest" extreme, just visit Disney World!***

SOURCES

Associations

United States

American Association of Botanical Associations and Arboreta
786 Church Road
Wayne, PA 19087-4713

American Association of Nurserymen
1250 I St. NW
Washington, DC 20036

American Conifer Society National Office
P.O. Box 314
Perry Hall, MD 21128
(410) 256-5595

American Herb Association
P.O. Box 353
Rescue, CA 95672

American Herb Society
P.O. Box 1673
Nevada City, CA 95959

American Horticultural Society
7931 East Boulevard Drive
Alexandria, VA 22308-1300

American Hosta Society
7802 NE 63rd Street
Vancouver, WA 98662

American Rock Garden Society
P.O. Box 67
Millwood, NY 10546

American Rose Society
P.O. Box 30,000
Shreveport, LA 71130-0030
(318) 938-5402

American Society of Landscape Architects
4401 Connecticut Ave., NW, 5th floor
Washington, DC 20008

Asssociated Landscape Contractors of America
12200 Sunrise Valley Drive, Suite 150
Reston, VA 22091

Herb Society of America
9019 Kirtland Chardon Road
Mentor, OH 44060
(216) 256-0514

Heritage Rose Foundation
1512 Gormon Street
Raleigh, NC 7606

Heritage Rose Group
925 Galvin Drive
El Cerrito, CA 94530

International Bulb Society
P.O. Box 4928
Culver City, CA 90230

International Society of Arboriculture
6 Dunlap Court
P.O. Box 66
Savoy, IL 61874

International Water Lily Society
Santa Barbara Botanic Gardens
1212 Mission Canyon Road
Santa Barbara, CA 93105
(805) 682-4726

National Arborist Association
Rt. 101, P.O. Box 19004
Amherst, NH 03031-1904

Plant Amnesty
906 NW 87th Street
Seattle, WA 98117

Pond Society
P.O. Box 449
Acworth, GA 30101

Canada

Alpine Garden Club of British Columbia
Box 5161-MPO
Vancouver, BC V6B 4B2

Canadian Rose Society
10 Fairfax Crest
Scarborough, ON M1L 1Z8

Canadian Society of Landscape Architects
306 Metcalfe Street
Ottawa, ON K2P 1S2

Newfoundland Alpine & Rock Garden Club
Memorial University Botanical Garden,
University of Newfoundland
St. John's NF A1C 5S7

Ontario Herbalists Association
7 Alpine Avenue
Toronto, ON M6P 3R6

Ontario Rock Garden Society
Box 146
Shelburne, ON L0N 1S0

Plant Sources

United States

Ambergate Gardens
8015 Krey Avenue
Waconia, MN 55387
(612) 443-2248
Perennials and grasses

Andre Viette Farm & Nursery
P.O. Box 1109
Fishersville, VA 22939
(540) 943-2315
Grasses, hostas, perennials

The Antique Rose Emporium
Rt. 5, Box 143
Brenham, TX 77833
(800) 441-0002
Roses

Banyai Hostas
11 Gates Circle
Hockessin, DE 19707
(302) 239-0887
Hostas

Bijou Alpines
P.O. Box 1252
Graham, WA 98338-8615
(360) 893-6191
Alpines, conifers, trees, perennials

Bluestone Perennials
7211 Middle Ridge Rd.
Madison, OH 44057
(800) 852-5243
Grasses, perennials, trees

Bridgewood Gardens
P.O. Box 800
Crownsville, MD 21032
(410) 849-3916
Hostas

Burpee
300 Park Avenue
Warminster, PA 18974
Annuals, perennials, vegetables, herbs

Busse Gardens
5873 Oliver Avenue SW
Cokato, MN 55321
(320) 286-2654
Grasses, perennials, hostas

Carrol Gardens
444 East Main Street
PO Box 310H
Westminster, MD 21157
Hostas, herbs, perennials, trees

Classic Groundcovers
405 Belmont Road
Athens, GA 30605-4905
(800) 248-8424
Grasses, perennials

Clifford's Perennial & Vine
Route 2, Box 320
East Troy, WI 53120
(414) 968-5525
Perennials, trees

Davidson-Wilson Greenhouses, Inc.
R.R. 2, Box 168, Department 11
Crawfordsville, IN 47933-9426
(317) 364-0556
Herbs

Englearth Gardens
2461 22nd Street
Hopkins, MI 49328
(616) 793-7196
Hostas, perennials

Ferry-Morse Seeds
P.O. Box 488
Fulton, KY 42041-0488
Vegetables, herbs

Foliage Gardens
2003 128th Avenue, S.E.
Bellevue, WA 98005
(206) 747-2998
Trees, ferns, Japanese maples

Gilson Gardens
P.O. Box 277
3059 US Route 20
Perry OH 44081
(216) 259-2378
Conifers, perennials, trees

A High Country Garden
2902 Rufina Street
Santa Fe, NM 87505-2929
(505) 438-3031
Grasses, perennials, cactuses

Homestead Division of Sunnybrook Famrs
9448 Mayfield Road
Chesterland, OH 44026
Hostas

Johnny's Selected Seeds
310 Foss Hill Road
Albion, ME 04910-9731
(207) 437-9294
Grasses, herbs, vegetables

J.W. Jung Seed Co.
335 S. High Street
Randolph, WI 53957-0001
(414) 326-3121
Bulbs, perennials, trees, vegetables

Klehm Nursery
4210 North Duncan Road
Champaign, IL 61821-9559
(800) 553-3715
Hostas, perennials

Kuk's Forest Nursery
10174 Barr Road
Brecksville, OH 44141-3302
(216) 526-5271
Hostas

Kurt Bluemel, Inc.
2740 Greene Lane
Baldwin, MD 21013-9523
(410) 557-7229
Hostas, perennials

Lamb Nurseries
101 East Sharp Avenue
Spokane, WA 99202
(509) 328-7956
Grasses, perennials, trees

Lilypons Water Gardens
P.O. Box 10
Buckeystown, MD 21707-0010
(800) 999-5459
Water plants and accessories

McClure & Zimmerman
108 W. Winnebago Street
P.O. Box 368
Friesland, WI 53935-0368
(414) 326-4220
Bulbs

Milaeger's Gardens
4838 Douglas Avenue
Racine, WI 53402-2498
(800) 669-9956
Grasses, perennials

Niche Gardens
1111 Dawson Rd.
Chapel Hill, NC 27516
(919) 967-0078
Perennials, trees

Paradise Water Gardens
14 May Street
Whitman MA 02382
(617) 447-4711, 447-8595
Water plants and supplies

Plant Delights Nursery
9241 Sauls Road
Raleigh, NC 27603
(919) 772-4794
Conifers, grasses, hostas, perennials, trees

Porterhowse Farms
41370 S.E. Thomas Road
Sandy, OR 97055
(503) 668-5834
Conifers, perennials, trees

Powell's Gardens
9468 U.S. Highway 70 East
Princeton, NC 27569
(919) 936-4421
Hostas, conifers, perennials, trees

Prairie Nursery
P.O. Box 306
Westfield, WI 53964
(608) 296-3679
Grasses, wildflowers

Prairie Ridge Nursery
9738 Overland Road
Mt. Horeb, WI 53572-2832
(608) 437-5245
Grasses, perennials, wildflowers

Rare Conifer Nusery (of the Rare Conifer Foundation)
P.O. Box 100
Potter Valley, CA 95469
(707) 462-8068
Conifers, trees

Rock Spray Nursery, Inc.
P.O. Box 693
Truro, MA 02666-0693

Roses of Yesterday and Today
802 Brown's Valley Road
Watsonville, CA 95076-0398
(408) 724-2755, 724-3537
Roses

Savory's Gardens, Inc.
5300 Whiting Avenue
Edina, MN 55439-1249
(612) 941-8755
Hostas

Shady Oaks Nursery
112 10th Ave. SE
Waseca, MN 56093
(507) 835-5033
Grasses, hostas, perennials

Shepherd's Garden Seeds
6116 Highway 9
Felton, CA 95018
(408) 335-6910
Herbs, vegetables

Shooting Star Nursery
444 Bates Road
Frankfort, KY 40601
(502) 223-1679
Grasses, perennials, water plants

Siskiyou Rare Plant Nursery
Dept. 72, 2825 Cummings Rd.
Medford, OR 97501
(541) 772-6846
Conifers, perennials, trees

Slocum Water Gardens
1101 Cypress Gardens Blvd.
Winter Haven, FL 33884-1932
(941) 293-7151
Water plants and supplies

Southern Perennials & Herbs
98 Bridges Road
Tylertown, MS 39667
(601) 684-1769
Herbs, perennials

Stark Bro.'s
P.O. Box 10
Louisiana, MO 63353-0010
(800) 325-4180
Conifers, trees

Surry Gardens
P.O. Box 145, Route 172
Surry, ME 04684
(207) 667-4493
Grasses, perennials

The Thomas Jefferson Center for Historic Plants at Monticello
P.O. Box 316
Charlottesville, VA 22902-0316
(804) 984-9822
Heirloom plants

Thompson and Morgan, Inc.
P.O. Box 1308
Jackson, NJ 08527-0308
(800) 274-7333
Grasses, vegetables

Tradewinds Bamboo Nursery
28446 Hunter Creek Loop
Gold Beach, OR 97444
(541) 247-0835
Grasses and bamboos

Van Dyck's Flower Farms, Inc.
P.O. Box 430
Brightwaters, NY 11718-0430
(800) 248-2852
Bulbs

Van Ness Water Gardens
2460 North Euclid Ave.
Upland, CA 91784-1199
(909) 982-2425
Water plants and supplies

Waterford Gardens
74 East Allendale Road
P.O. Box 389
Saddle River, NJ 07458
(201) 327-0721
Water plants and supplies

Wayside Gardens
1 Garden Lane
Hodges, SC 29695-0001
(800) 845-1124
Perennials, grasses

White Flower Farm, Plantsmen
P.O. Box 50
Litchfield, CT 06759-0050
(860) 496-9624
Grasses, perennials

Woodlanders, Inc.
1128 Colleton Ave.
Aiken, SC 29801
(803) 648-7522

Canada

Corn Hill Nursery Ltd.
RR 5
Petitcodiac NB EOA 2HO
(506) 756-3635, 756-1087

Ferncliff Gardens
SS 1
Mission, British Columbia
V2V 5V6

Hortico, Inc.
723 Robson Road
Waterdown, Ontario L0R 2H1
(905) 689-6984

McFayden Seed Co.
30 Ninth Street, Suite 200
Brandon, Manitoba CA R7A 6N4

Stirling Perennials
RR 1
Morpeth, Ontario
N0P 1X0

Australia

Country Farm Perennials
RSD Laings Road
Nayook VIC 3821

Cox's Nursery
RMB 216 Oaks Road
Thrilmere NSW 2572

Honeysuckle Cottage Nursery
Lot 35 Bowen Mountain Road
Bowen Mountain via Grosevale NSW 2753

Swan Bros Pty Ltd
490 Galston Road
Dural NSW 2158

Further Reading

General

All About Pruning by Fred K. Buscher

Burpee Seed Starter by Maureen Heffernan

The Complete Book of Plant Propagation Charles W. Heuser, editor

The Complete Guide to Foliage Planting by Sandra Bond and C.J. Taylor

Creative Propagation: A Grower's Guide by Peter Thompson

Foliage Plants by Ursula Buchan

Gardening with Foliage Plants: Leaf, Bark, and Berry by Ethne Clarke

Growing Plants from Seed by John Kelly

The New Seed Starter's Handbook by Nancy Bubel

Pruning Made Easy by Lewis Hill

Pruning Ornamental Shrubs and Trees by L.F. Eager

Secrets of Plant Propagation by Lewis Hill

Conifers

Conifers: The Illustrated Encyclopedia by D.M. van Gelderen and J.R.P.van Hoey Smith

Conifers for Your Garden by Adrian Bloom

Garden Conifers in Colour by Brian Proudley and Valerie Proudley

A Garden of Conifers: Introduction and Selection Guide by Robert A. Obrizok

Growing Conifers: Brooklyn Botanic Garden Handbook

How to Grow Conifers by Brian Proudley

Identifying Ornamental Conifers by Richard Bird

Know Your Conifers by Herbert L. Edlin

Manual of Cultivated Conifers by P. Ouden

The Pruning of Trees, Shrubs, and Conifers by George E. Brown and updated by John Bryan.

Grasses and Bamboos

American Bamboos by Emmet J. Judziewicz

Bamboos by Christine Recht and Max F. Wetterwald.

The Book of Bamboo by David Farrelly

Encyclopedia of Ornamental Grasses by John Greenlee and Derek Fell

Gardening with Grasses by Michael King

Grasses: An Identification Guide by Lauren Brown

Manual of Grasses with Rick Darke, consulting editor

Ornamental Grass Gardening: Design, Ideas, Function, and Effects by Reinhardt, Reinhardt, and Moskowitz

Ornamental Grasses, Bamboos, Rushes and Sedges by J. Taylor Nigel

Ornamental Grasses: Brooklyn Botanic Garden Handbook

Plantfinder's Guide to Ornamental Grasses by Roger Grounds

Hostas

The Gardener's Guide to Growing Hostas by Diana Grenfell

Genus Hosta by W. George Schmid

Hosta: The Flowering Foliage Plant by Diana Grenfell

The Hosta Book, Paul Aden, editor

Hostas by Andrew Mikolajski

Hostas: Foliage Plants in Garden Design by Sandra Bond

Trees and Shrubs

The 100 Best Trees and Shrubs by Elvin McDonald

The Complete Book of Shrubs by Kim E. Tripp

Easy, Practical Pruning: Techniques for Training Trees, Shrubs, Vines, and Roses by Barbara Ellis and Frances Tenenbaum

Garden Shrubs by Arthur Hellyer

The Gardener's Essential Plant Guide: Over 4,000 Varieties of Garden Plants Including Trees, Shrubs, and Vines by Brian Davis

Ornamental Shrubs, Climbers, and Bamboos by Graham Stuart Thomas

Principles and Practices of Planting Trees and Shrubs by Gary W. Watson and E.B. Himelick

Shrubs: The New Glamour Plant, Bob Hyland and Janet Marinellim, editors

The Tree and Shrub Expert by Dr. D.G. Hessayon

The Year in Trees: Superb Woody Plants for Four-Season Gardens by Kim E. Tripp and J.C. Raulston

The Woodland Garden by Robert Gillmore and Eileen Octavec

Perennials

100 Favorite Perennials by Teri Dunn

550 Perennial Garden Ideas by Derek Fell

Ball Perennial Manual: Propagation and Production by Jim Nau

Caring for Perennials: What to Do and When to Do It by Janet MacUnovich

The Complete Book of Perennials by Graham Rice

Designing with Perennials by Pamela Harper

From Seed to Bloom: How to Grow over 500 Annuals, Perennials and Herbs by Eileen Powell

Gardening with Perennials Month by Month by Joseph Hudak

Landscaping with Perennials by Elizabeth Stell

Perennial Ground Covers by David S. MacKenzie

Taylor's Guide to Perennials by Norman Taylor

The Well-Tended Perennial Garden: Planting and Pruning Techniques by Tracy Disabato-Aust

PLANT HARDINESS ZONES

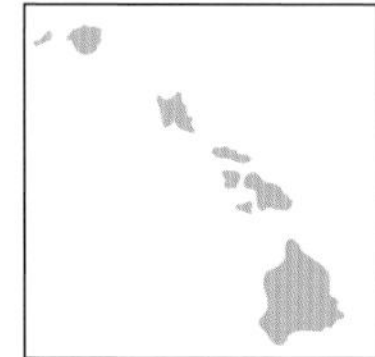

Range of Average Annual Minimum Temperatures for Each Zone

	Fahrenheit (°F)	Celsius (°C)
ZONE 1	BELOW -50°	BELOW -45.6°
ZONE 2	-50° TO -40°	-45.6° TO -40°
ZONE 3	-40° TO -30°	-40° TO -34.4°
ZONE 4	-30° TO -20°	-34.4° TO -28.9°
ZONE 5	-20° TO -10°	-28.9° TO -23.3°
ZONE 6	-10° TO 0°	-23.3° TO -17.8°
ZONE 7	0° TO 10°	-17.8° TO -12.2°
ZONE 8	10° TO 20°	-12.2° TO -6.7°
ZONE 9	20° TO 30°	-6.7° TO -1.1°
ZONE 10	30° TO 40°	-1.1° TO 4.4°
ZONE 11	ABOVE 40°	ABOVE 4.4°

If you are living outside North America, use the chart to determine your Plant Hardiness Zone.

INDEX

Photography Credits

©David Cavagnaro: pp. 11 top, 17, 21 right, 29, 38–39, 52–53, 57 top, 57 bottom, 96, 97, 100–101, 104–105, 107, 108, 110, 122–123, 125, 127 left, 129

©R. Todd Davis: pp. 5, 7, 20, 21 left, 22, 23 bottom, 34 bottom, 36 left, 40, 46, 55, 67, 75, 94–95, 111 top

©Derek Fell: pp. 2, 12 left, 16, 34 top, 45 top, 47, 60, 63, 65, 70–71, 73, 79, 91, 98, 99 top, 99 bottom, 102, 112–113, 114, 115

©John Glover: pp. 14 left, 15, 27 bottom right, 28 top, 36–37, 54, 56, 58–59, 59 right, 82–83, 85, 106, 124, 130, 131

©Dency Kane: pp. 8–9, 48–49, 66, 68–69, 81 top right, 92–93, 102–103, 109, 111 bottom, 116–117, 118, 128

©Charles Mann: pp. 14 center, 23 top, 28 bottom, 32, 45 bottom, 61, 80 center left, 80–81, 86, 89, 113 right, 119, 132–133

©Clive Nichols: pp. 1, 26–27, 35, 41, 77, 87, 90, 103, 120–121

©Jerry Pavia: pp. 12 right, 14 right, 24–25, 34 center, 44, 45 top, 50–51, 78, 84, 88, 101 bottom right, 126, 127 right

Visuals Unlimited: ©Gary W. Carter: p. 33 bottom; ©Ross Frid: p. 33 top; ©John Gerlach: p. 11 bottom; ©Gary Meszaros: p. 13

Illustrations by Jennifer Markson: pp. 18–19, 31, 42–43, 48–49, 64, 76